Dressing
for
Glamour

Michael Childers

John Engstead

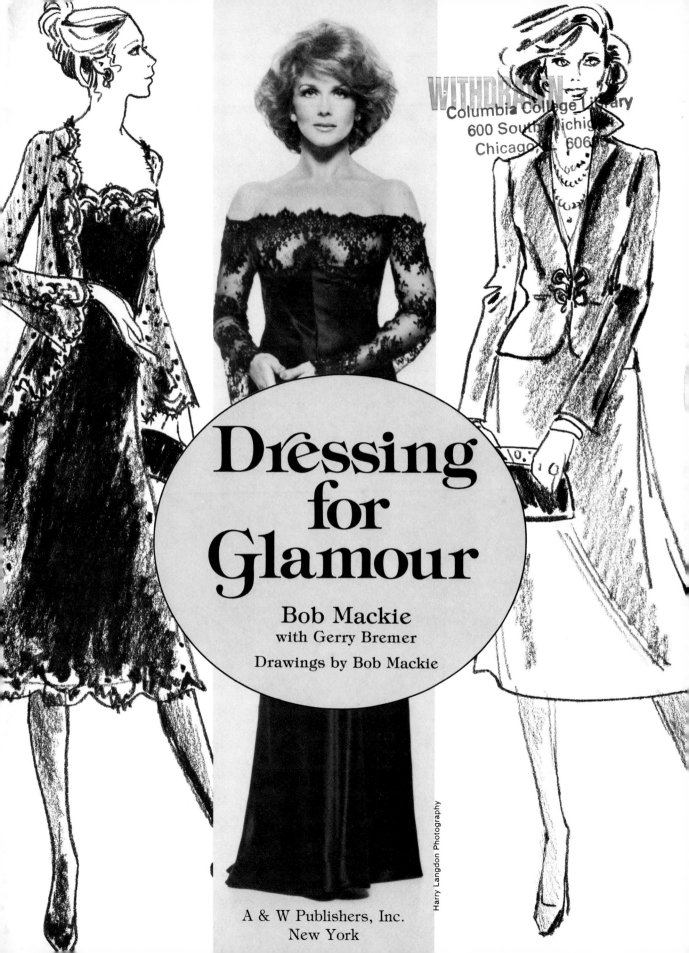

Dressing for Glamour

Bob Mackie
with Gerry Bremer

Drawings by Bob Mackie

Harry Langdon Photography

A & W Publishers, Inc.
New York

So many people helped to make this book possible. A very special thanks to: the staff of Elizabeth Courtney Costumes; the Fashion Institute of Design and Merchandising; Marge Plecher, who kept it all together; Jef Billings, for his creative contributions; Estelle Lawrence, because we promised her!

For Elizabeth and all my ladies

Copyright © 1979 by Bob Mackie and Gerry Bremer

Published by
A & W Publishers, Inc.
95 Madison Avenue
New York, New York 10016

Library of Congress Cataloging in Publication Data

Mackie, Bob.
    Dressing for glamour.

    1. Clothing and dress.   I. Title.
TT507.M3413   746.9'2   79-14907
ISBN 0-89479-053-6

Designed by Marcia Ben-Eli
Printed in the United States of America

CONTENTS

FOREWORD

by Carol Burnett

When I was a little girl, I used to think a costume designer thought up a pretty dress for Lana Turner, drew a picture on a piece of paper, colored it with crayons and turned it over to someone who could sew. Maybe that still happens in some cases, but not with Bob Mackie.

Bob started working with me in 1967 when our show first went on the air. He was around ten-years old at the time (because now, twelve years later, he doesn't look more than twenty-two), but beneath that youthful exterior and little boy smile is the heart and soul of a perfectionist and taskmaster.

He has designed and executed—seen personally to the construction of—over 1800 costumes for our show alone. This includes not only the costumes I wore, but every single piece of clothing that appeared on the screen! All were designed, coordinated and overseen by him. That's a lot of hours and manual labor.

But his true genius lies in his zeal for detail—and his sense of humor.

I'll go on record by saying he has saved many a comedy sketch with some of the outrageously funny getups he cooked up for me and others. There were many times when I didn't "find" my character until I saw what Bob had in mind for her attire.

To name a few:

Mrs. Wiggins: That black skirt should be featured in *Architectural Digest*.

Nora Desmond: Not only did he design the costume, but he thought up the make-up and designed the wig. (Incidentally, he designed all our wigs, and then they were executed by Roselle Friedland.)

The Fat Lady: A masterpiece of flesh tones and blubber, plus a belly button.

Zelda the Nag: The uglier she was, the better we liked her.

Eunice: That same, poor, awful print dress with the over permanented hair. No wonder she's such a loser.

There are hundreds more!

The key to Bob's success, I think, is that he has a producer's mind. He doesn't just think of his department alone. He looks at every show as a whole. He reads and studies the script as much as I do. He *knows* the characters before he sets his pencil to his sketch pad.

He's tops in his field now, but I won't be a bit surprised when he branches out into other areas and reaches even greater heights.

He's nice.

He's brilliant.

And I love him.

Carol Burnett

PART ONE

Behind the Glitter

Letters arrive each day. They come from children so young that mothers have to write for them. They come from students, from fans and from the casually curious; from every state and every country. The mailman brings sketches in battered brown envelopes depicting costumes designed especially for favorite personalities. Some send appeals for an analysis of their work. Others, more confident, request that checks be sent by return mail.

My favorite correspondent is a fifty-year-old man who has spent a lifetime working in a restaurant. He is convinced that now is the time to switch careers, and nothing I say will separate him from his dream—to design glamourous gowns for beautiful women. It's his dream and he's sticking with it.

The letters are filled with questions. How can I become a costume designer? Can you tell me something about Cher? Carol? Mitzi or Raquel?

The writers are curious about those people whose names conjure up visions of glamourous magic. They want to know who lives behind those glittery, mysterious facades that invade their living rooms seven nights a week. There are requests for tips on how to follow in my footsteps, applications from aspiring young designers who would like to be my apprentice and letters from those who just want to learn something, anything at all, about the fascinating, frantic world in which I live and work.

Each letter receives a reply. Most demand an answer because they are are so filled with hope and expectations. The writers of these letters are anxious for any tidbit I might offer that will give some concrete support for their dreams.

This book is my chance to answer those questions. By writing in the first person, I can speak on a one-to-one basis, as I never could do otherwise.

If you would like more than anything else in the world to become a costume designer, I trust this will serve as an inspiration and a guide. If you only wish to share an intimate glimpse behind the scenes, to become better acquainted with some of the stars whose faces are more familair than members of your own family, I will introduce you to my life and to the stars as I know them.

I may disappoint you, however, if it is gossip you are looking forward to. It is not my intention to air for public entertainment the private lives of the celebrities. But I do want you to meet the stars with whom I work, the dedicated entertainers who put in long, grueling hours, days on end, in order to bring us laughter, music and escape—however, brief—from the tension-filled world in which we live.

I believe you will like these real, flesh-and-blood people who shine through the fabulous facades. The famous are (to repeat a trite, but true, phrase) just like you and me, *except* for that elusive, very important difference: They are glamourous! Perhaps we can define together exactly what that glamour is, and maybe a little of it will rub off.

"Fair Cher" and friend.

CHAPTER ONE

Getting From There to Here

"I know what I'm going to be when I grow up!" Most of us have said that. The very young have strong notions about their future careers. Firemen, nurses and airplane pilots were big when I was a kid. But I have little doubt that today's young dreamers—thanks to television—are somewhat more sophisticated and that yesterday's idols have been superseded by the likes of space explorers and lady presidents.

We had no television in our home when I was a kid, but there were movies, and for me that's where it all began. There was nothing I liked better than watching a musical at the neighborhood theater, completely involved with all the color, flash and glitter. I was only five years old at the time and, while I didn't really understand what was happening on the screen, I wanted more than anything else to be part of the glamourous, magical world that was so far removed from anything I had ever known. I had to be a part of that wonderful world.

As dreams go, mine wasn't so unusual. But for me, it turned out to be something special.

To this day I can recall the thrill of watching the *Ziegfeld Follies*, the colorful charm of *Meet Me In St. Louis* and those exotic films starring Carmen Miranda, who had more "stuff" on her than I could ever have imagined. I think back on it now and realize that it was all that "stuff" that really got to me.

How could I ever forget Betty Grable, with her silky blonde hair, arrayed in those flashy pink and turquoise costumes with matching furs? To me, Betty was the epitome of loveliness, too beautiful to be real. She remained my favorite until a few years later when Marilyn Monroe shimmered across the screen and became the woman in my life. As I grew older and more sophisticated, my interest in lusty, busty

blonds began to wane. Along came Audrey Hepburn. She had such style and elegance that the others paled in comparison. She was a true lady.

When I was about ten, a very special motion picture came along and gave a new direction to my life. With its famous ballet sequence, *An American in Paris* so totally captured my imagination that for the first time in my life I became acutely aware of the importance of costume designing and the contribution it made to the overall effect of the film.

After sitting through several performances I did something I had never done before, I read the credits: "Costumes designed by Irene Sharaff." It was a name I was to see over and over again, invariably associated with the most elegant and glamourous costumes. My admiration for her work had a lot to do with my ultimate decision to become a costume designer.

I began sketching. I lived with my grandparents and there were few children in our neighborhood, so I spent a great deal of time by myself. Drawing increasingly became my main preoccupation. It kept me quiet for hours on end. Most of my drawings were small figures of people lavishly dressed in fancy clothing. Each figure represented an actual person in my life, and I carefully initialed each one.

Since my pastime kept me from disrupting an orderly household, I received a lot of support in the form of paper and crayons. But, after a while, merely drawing the small figures was not enough. Inspired by the movies, I began to put together entire sets consisting of elaborate scenery to go with the lavish costumes. After sketching each item, I would cut it out and assemble everything on my dresser, which soon became a permanent stage.

To achieve the right mood for each performance, I'd play a current record. When all was in readiness, the overhead light was turned off, and, with the aid of my flashlight, I'd spotlight the scene and admire my handiwork. I was primarily interested in the visual effect and would no sooner have one production completed than I would dismantle the entire project and begin on something new.

Recently, when I came across a large folder filled with those early creations, I discovered the importance of that period of my life. It had set the stage for the rest of my life.

Had it not been for my grandmother's preoccupation with fresh air, life would have been serene. But she would worry endlessly at my stubborn refusal to exchange the privacy of my room for southern California's great outdoors, and, in an attempt to remedy this situation, she would periodically order me to the front porch and lock the door behind me. No amount of pleading or tears would make her relent until she was satisfied I had inhaled enough fresh air for the day.

Early inspiration: Bobby Mackie.

Later fulfillment: Cher.

John Engstead

Photo courtesy of NBC

(Above) Lee Remick was a saucy centerpiece for the first show in "Danny Thomas' Wonderful World of Burlesque" series that Ray Aghayan and I designed in the mid-sixties. (Right) Carol Channing as Lorelei Lee in Lorelei, the updated version of Gentlemen Prefer Blondes.

Photo by Seawell

"Alice Through the Looking Glass" was the first TV show to receive an Emmy award for costume design. The show starred (clockwise) Jimmy Durante as Humpty Dumpty; Judy Rolin as Alice; Robert Coote as the Red King, Nanette Fabray as the White Queen, Agnes Moorehead as the Red Queen, Ricardo Montalban as the White King; and Jack Palance as the evil Jabberwock.

Posing with Carol Burnett in 1967, the first year of her very successful comedy-variety series.

High school broke the pattern of my isolated existence. For the first time reality replaced make-believe as a top interest for me. My fellow students took the parts of the paper people and a real stage replaced the dresser top.

I was then living with my father in Rosemead, a Los Angeles suburb, where, fortunately for me, the school was blessed with an excellent and very active drama department. The head of the department, a wonderfully perceptive and talented man named Peter Mauk, became my mentor. I, in turn, became his star pupil. I took over the leads in school plays, designed the costumes and helped create the sets.

My designs didn't reach the stage in their pure form. The mothers who were recruited to do the sewing were far more concerned with upholding their daughters' modesty than they were in following my somewhat skimpy designs. As a result, every neckline was invariably raised three inches or a large piece of feathers or fur was added.

But it didn't really matter, for almost overnight I had been catapulted into the exhilarating world of the theater, able to play out my fantasies to the fullest. In the process I paid no attention to academic subjects, such as algebra and geometry. It was far more important, after all, to plan who would be wearing what in an upcoming school play than it was to attempt to cope with the intricacies of Pythagoras and his theorem.

My obsession with costumes and clothing at this time made me aware of the importance of being well dressed. But that meant having to earn money. My options were limited in that direction—washing dishes or mowing lawns. I chose the latter and every weekend I would cart my father's heavy iron mower from door to door, mowing crabgrass lawns and collecting more calluses than coins in the process. To this day the smell of freshly cut grass makes me shudder.

Fortunately, for the sake of my fingers and finances both, more lucrative job opportunities presented themselves as I grew older. During my senior year in high school, I found a part-time job as a copy boy in the advertising department of a major Los Angeles department store. It was a job made to order.

While running errands to various buyers' offices throughout the store, I was able to check out the new merchandise as it arrived in all the departments. These constant trips also gave me a chance to observe the various kinds of people who patronized the store. Later, when costuming characters for movies or television shows, I was able to recall some of those richly colorful types.

In time my responsibilities expanded. I became the store's Easter Bunny, its Back-to-School Clown and its Space Man. (I lost out on the Santa role; I was informed that I was not the jolly old St. Nick type.) Then, one day, the display director discovered my sketching abilities. I was put to work hand-lettering signs, and, shortly thereafter, my creative talents were given free reign when I was asked to paint a small mural for the children's department.

Life continued in this fashion. After graduation I enrolled in Pasadena City College as an advertising art and illustration major and quit my department store job with every intention of devoting my energies to studying. But I couldn't resist the temptation when the store called and invited me back as a free-lance artist at eight dollars per hour. It was quite a promotion from the dollar twenty-five I had previously earned.

The two years at Pasadena allowed me to build a good portfolio, which I then used to apply for a scholarship at Chouinard Art Institute. At that time it was the finest school of its kind on the West Coast. The minute I was admitted as an advertising art student, I changed my major to costume design. Although the administration was dismayed, I was finally doing what I had always wanted to do—design costumes.

Always in need of ready cash, I took all sorts of strange jobs—courtesy of the school's placement service. Whenever there was a call for a sketch artist, I would be alerted. I was fast and I was willing to go anywhere. The work usually turned out well.

One of my first assignments was for a company who needed sketches for their mail-order catalog. It was the sixties and the Kennedys were riding the crest of their popularity, so I was instructed to make each voluptuous figure clad in erotic underwear look like The First Lady—from the neck up.

My next assignment was stranger still. Madame Exotica, an entertainer, called the school asking for someone capable of designing costumes for a nightclub act. I was sent to a rather sinister house in a seedy part of Venice, a small seaside community west of Los Angeles. I rang the doorbell and was greeted by a young man attired in an elegant crimson robe. He extended both arms in a gesture of welcome and exclaimed breathlessly, "Do come in. I am Madame Exotica."

Startled, confused and rapidly getting cold feet, I backed off, mumbling something about not being sufficiently qualified for the job. Ignoring my comments completely, my host grabbed me by the arm and dragged me into the house. Madame Exotica shoved me into a chair, picked up a beribboned tambourine and prepared to demonstrate his act. As I watched, with rounded eyes, dumbfounded, he shed his robe to reveal a practically nude body covered with gold glitter. Ignoring my misgivings and objections about the job, the sparkling figure whirled faster and faster about the room. Finally, I jumped up and ran. Even I didn't need the money that badly.

(Opposite) Ultraglamourous gowns designed at the age of fourteen. Simple, don't you think?

Betty

Not long after my meeting with Madame Exotica, I accepted my one and only job in the Los Angeles garment district. A local manufacturer was looking for someone to assist him in preparing a sample line. I had gone to him hoping he would buy some of the designs in my portfolio, but he wasn't interested. He was, however, delighted to have an eager young designer around, someone he could put to work. He suggested I try my hand at cutting samples. My complete lack of experience didn't bother him in the slightest, and, taking the scissors he handed me, I proceeded to cut the fabric.

By the end of my first week, I had learned two valuable lessons: One, the garment business wasn't my cup of tea, and two, merely drawing pretty pictures wasn't going to get me anywhere. My instructors at school had been right when they had insisted I buckle down and learn pattern drafting, draping and sewing. These were subjects I detested. To me they were no better than algebra and geometry. But I tried. To this day I am grateful to my teachers in those classes, Charles Teske and Jack Hanford, for pushing and cajoling me until I mastered the tools of my trade.

The highlight of the Chouinard School calendar was the Art Student's Ball, an annual event that was promoted to raise funds for the school. During my first year at Chouinard, I was put in charge of the costumes for the court, which meant I was to design a gown for the queen, among others. The theme that year was Grecian—elaborate Grecian.

Jayne Mansfield, the 1950s sex symbol, had offered her awesome presence in the role of the queen. I immediately decided to make the most of her not so inconsiderable attributes and proceeded to design a ball gown that would reveal as much of the royal body as possible. The project became an engineering as much as a design feat. I labored for hours in order to be able to cantilever the queen's bust as far out as it would go, while slitting the long skirt up the sides of both legs, also as far as possible.

Two weeks before the big event, Jayne Mansfield arrived on campus to have some publicity shots taken. She was conservatively dressed in a smart tweed suit and matching sweater. To create a look more appropriate for the situation, I was instructed to take a piece of the gold fabric from which I was making the royal gown and wrap it around the famous body.

The effect, over suit and sweater, left much to be desired. So Jayne elected to solve the problem in her own original fashion. Totally unperturbed, she asked me to hold the gold fabric in front of her while she peeled off all her clothing. Then she pushed her bust out as far as it would go and told me to pull the fabric as tightly as I could. All the while she dazzled the photographers with her smile.

By now the place was a bedlam, and news of it spread about the school like wildfire, and the entire student body was gathered to watch the proceedings. Fully aware of the activity going on behind the golden cloth I was holding, the students cheered me on with an enthusiasm only college students have.

A week later, Mr. Teske and I drove to the Mansfield mansion for a final fitting. Jayne and her husband, muscle man Mickey Hargitay, lived in a pseudo-Mediterranean pink Hollywood palace on Sunset Boulevard. It was complemented by a heart-shaped swimming pool and was decorated inside completely in pinks and whites.

Asked to remove my shoes to keep from soiling the thick pink carpet, I was shown into the master bedroom, which was dominated by an enormous bed, also heart-shaped. Making a grand entrance, Jayne and Mickey emerged from their steamy, pink, fur-lined bathroom, damp and glowing. They seemed totally oblivious to the shock waves they were creating upon me. Mickey was to be his wife's escort at the ball, and both were fitted in the costumes we had brought along.

This was a rather memorable moment in my early career. I often wonder if Jayne should be considered the first star I ever dressed or the first I ever undressed?

Unique as it was, my experience with Jayne Mansfield was one of many that would eventually lead to a better understanding of and a fresher outlook on the business of which I had chosen to become a part. Another of these unique experiences had to do with an opposite aspect of the film world, the studios of Walt Disney.

Walt Disney was one of the school's benefactors, and the wife of one of Disney's top executives was a member of the Chouinard board of directors. She learned that I was having problems locating some items for another project I was doing, so she suggested that we take a trip to the Disney wardrobe department and see what we could find. I was delighted and accepted the invitation to join her and her husband for lunch prior to our planned studio visit. It was, unfortunately, my first exposure to what has since become known as "the three-martini lunch." It was, in fact, my first exposure to a martini of any kind.

Would I like a drink? Sure. And when the watery-looking liquid arrived, I had no problem whatsoever in downing it. It was easy, also, to down rounds two and three. Needless to say, I have no recollection of leaving the restaurant. Furthermore, I was convinced I had shattered my carefully cultivated professional image. My reputation didn't suffer any permanent damage, but I have often wondered if the reason I was never asked to do any work for the Disney people stemmed from that wonderful three martini lunch.

In addition to the ball Chouinard put on an annual fashion show to give students the opportunity to present their work to members of the industry and press. It was an important event, one for which we

Carmen

prepared for months.

Lack of money precluded the hiring of professional models, so each student was responsible for finding someone to model his or her entries. I can recall each year haunting the halls for weeks, leering at every girl in sight, speculating on the type of body hiding beneath the grubby dungarees. Since I did, even then, expose a large amount of skin with my designs, finding the best possible body was very important.

There came a time when I myself was asked to be one of the models. One year, the night before the fashion show, I was asked by a fellow student to model his swim wear. Upon studying my fish-belly white complexion in the mirror, I felt I had to do something about it. I hurried to the nearest drugstore to purchase some instant tanning lotion. It would, said the bottle, turn me into a healthy-looking, bronze Adonis overnight. It was late when I returned to my room, the light was poor and I was dead tired. Nevertheless, I stripped down, coated myself with the magic fluid from top to bottom and fell into bed.

The morning light revealed that I possessed a rather bilious-looking orange body, instead of the promised glowing tan, and there was no time to repair the damage. Soap and water only made matters worse. I ended up making my modeling debut looking to all the world like a poorly painted cigar store Indian.

Two of the happiest years of my life were spent at Chouinard for I was doing what I loved most. I was also fortunate enough to win several honors and awards. But, when the school offered to extend my scholarship for an additional year, I declined with thanks. I was convinced there was nothing further I could learn in school and was ready to face the world.

As it turned out, the world of design wasn't really ready for me. For six months, portfolio firmly clamped under one arm, I pounded the pavements, knocking on doors and sitting in reception rooms, hoping someone would give me The Big Break. From 8:00 P.M. until midnight I washed dishes at *The Nine Muses*, a restaurant with a wonderful ambiance, excellent food and the lowest prices in Los Angeles. Jamila, who owned and ran the place with her husband, Satya, was an artistic soul. (She ultimately gave up cooking for belly dancing.) She could not stand sharing her kitchen with anyone with whom she was not artistically compatible. Like the customers who frequented the restaurant, the dishwasher, too, had to be artistic. That was how I got the job.

The Nine Muses had two specialties, Indian curry and various Italian dishes, so the suds in which I labored were tinted a sickly curry yellow and dirty tomato red. But with the job came plenty of good food, wonderful company and, best of all, lots of free time to pursue bigger and better things, although I was beginning to doubt whether they were ever going to happen.

Then, one day, that long awaited phone call arrived. I was summoned to Paramount Studios, where Frank Thompson was in charge of designing the wardrobe for a film entitled *Love Is a Ball*, starring Hope Lange, Glenn Ford and Charles Boyer.

Frank needed someone to sketch the men's clothes. Drawing men was not his forte. It was not mine either, but I wasn't going to lose this golden opportunity by admitting my weakness.

The men I sketched did end up looking rather strange, but no one seemed to mind, and, before long, I found myself sketching some of the women's clothes as well. My salary was a terrific $125 per week, which was more money than I had ever made.

I joined the Costume Designers' Guild and for the first time I felt like a true professional, even though I was only an associate member. Edith Head, who was then Paramount's top designer in residence, would stop by from time to time to see how I was getting along. While making my rounds in search of a job, I had stopped in to see her several times. She had no openings at those times, but was unfailingly gracious and encouraging. She must have liked my work for, ultimately, she hired me to work for her.

When my job with Frank Thompson came to an end, I went to work for Jean Louis, who was preparing the gowns for Marilyn Monroe's *Something's Got to Give*, the ill-fated picture that was halted and left unfinished at Marilyn's untimely death. Not exactly Mr. Louis' first choice, I got the job because the sketch artist he really wanted was unavailable. It was a difficult apprenticeship; only after working steadily from morning until night for two weeks did I finally manage to come up with a sketch that was deemed worthy for the eyes of George Cukor, the director of the film.

It was customary for beginners to work behind the scenes, and, as a result, I never caught a glimpse of Marilyn or any of the other famous persons in the film. Mr. Louis always took the costumes to the stars so they could be fitted in the privacy of their dressing rooms. Needless to say, I was not invited to accompany him on those trips. Yet, the knowledge that some of the clothes I was sketching would one day be worn by some glamourous star seen by millions was enough incentive to keep me going.

After Jean Louis, I returned to Paramount to work with Edith Head. Still banished to the back room, I did happen to glance up one day from my sketch board to see Judy Garland sauntering down the hall. Unable to believe my eyes, I jumped up and made it to my open doorway just in time to see her disappear into the ladies' room. Since I was working in the women's wardrobe department, there were no separate facilities for men, and so I was able to brag to my friends that Judy and I shared the same john. That was as close as I ever got to

Queen Jayne

the performers in those days.

Though I had learned a lot from Jean Louis, working for Edith Head was far more exciting. She always had four or five projects going on at the same time, and, little by little, I managed to meet some of the stars as they came to her for fittings. My lunch hours were spent sneaking onto sound stages to watch the movies being made.

I quickly established a reputation for drawing flamboyant costumes, and, because of this, I missed out on a job I really wanted. The studio was preparing a film to star Dean Martin and Elizabeth Montgomery. A newcomer from television named Carol Burnett, of whom nobody in the wardrobe department had ever heard, was also to be in the film.

I had admired Carol for her work on "The Garry Moore Show," and, more than anything else, I wanted the opportunity to sketch her wardrobe for the movie. But I was already known for flash and Carol's role called for simple, tailored dresses. Someone else was assigned to work with her, and, to add insult to injury, I never even had the chance to meet her. But that would come later.

My first television job was as assistant to Ray Aghayan, who was then the designer for "The Judy Garland Show." Judy had a difficult figure to dress. Even though she was thin at the time, she had a short body, full bust, broad shoulders and skinny legs. But Judy adored clothes and loved nothing more than dressing up. We became good friends. I never saw the side of her that is written about so frequently, the temperamental prima donna who drove everyone to distraction with her moods and tantrums. My memories of Judy Garland are of a wonderfully warm human being who wore clothes with great style and never lost her sense of humor. I spent many evenings at her home, with friends and co-workers, laughing at her numerous amusing stories about Louis B. Mayer and his cohorts at MGM.

For a long time, Judy had difficulty remembering my name. I was always "that nice young man, what's his name?" It was still a far cry, however, from seeing her run to the ladies' room at Paramount.

It was at Judy's house that I met Judy's daughter Liza Minnelli, then seventeen. She had lots of stringy hair and loved to dance and sing. Liza had not yet developed a style of her own and was just a bundle of energy with a great deal of show biz savvy. I have enjoyed watching her grow into the amazing and talented performer she has become.

I received my first screen credit for my work on the "Judy Garland Show" and also established a long working relationship with my partner, Ray Aghayan. It was certainly a turning point in my career, and I will always be grateful for the experience. It wasn't, however, until I began working on my own that people began to accept and recognize me as a designer.

(Opposite) Judy Garland on her 1963 TV series.

Photo by Roddy McDowall

It was at the age of twenty-three that I was asked to design the costumes for a Dinah Shore special. But my age and youthful appearance seemed to be against me. One look was all Dinah needed to be convinced I could not possibly do an acceptable job.

Unfazed, I went ahead and created a wardrobe for her, which included a terrific looking pair of wide pants. It was long before that particular style became popular. Dinah took one look at my creations, tried them on, felt uncomfortable wearing them and threw the lot out in favor of a beaded dress she found in her closet. Since then Dinah and I have worked together several times and she has even worn the wide-legged pants.

My age continued to be a problem for me until the mid-sixties when the Beatles invaded America. Suddenly, being young was an asset. People everywhere were convinced that only the young knew what they were doing. Overnight I became that terrific young designer who could do no wrong. The phone started ringing regularly with more offers than I knew what to do with.

One of my first regular projects was "The King Family Show." I was able to design everything from gowns for the elegant ladies to diapers for the babies. In addition, Ray and I worked on many of the early Danny Thomas specials, which were especially exciting, for they gave me a chance to work with many different guest stars, including Lucille Ball, Cyd Charisse and Carol Channing.

One of the greatest thrills of my career happened at that time. We were asked to design costumes for a special entitled "Alice Through the Looking Glass," starring Nanette Fabray, Agnes Moorehead, Ricardo Montalban and Jack Palance. It was, to say the least, an unusual production. Many of the costumes we created for the show were made from foam rubber, a material that had rarely been used up to that time. For our efforts Ray and I received the 1967 Emmy Award for costume design, the first Emmy ever awarded in that category.

Mitzi Gaynor, a guest on one of the Danny Thomas specials, approached Ray about designing some costumes for her nightclub act. Unable to handle the project at that time, he recommended me. Mitzi agreed to take a chance on this young designer whom she had never met and, thus, became the first star to ask me to create her costumes.

Carol Burnett, the actress with whom I wanted to work so badly, caught Mitzi's act in Las Vegas and was impressed not only by the glamour, but also by the humorous touches I had created for Mitzi's act. As a result, Carol became my second big client. I started designing the clothes for her weekly comedy show soon thereafter. It was something I would continue to do for the next eleven years.

My work with Carol put me in constant contact with her numerous guest stars, among whom was Cher. . . . But more about her later.

All sorts of projects started to come along. In addition to television specials, I became involved with TV adaptations of such Broadway shows as *Kismet, Brigadoon* and *Carousel*. Somehow, these had to be sandwiched between Carol's weekly series and, later on, between Carol's show and "The Sonny & Cher Show."

I also continued creating Mitzi's wardrobe. In 1976 I designed a montage of twenties costumes for her, which brought me another Emmy for costume design.

My efforts during those years were concentrated on television, but I did take time out to work on several motion pictures. In 1972 Ray and I created the costumes for Diana Ross in *Lady Sings the Blues*, and in 1976 we designed all the costumes for *Funny Lady*, the film starring Barbra Streisand and James Caan. Both efforts netted us Academy Award nominations.

The opportunity to tackle one of the greatest challenges of my career came in 1973. Ray and I were asked to design a nightclub extravaganza planned for the opening of the MGM Grand Hotel in Las Vegas. "Hallelujah Hollywood" was to be the biggest, the most spectacular production of its kind ever attempted. Its theme was based on the old MGM musicals, a wonderful source of inspiration for such an overwhelming project. I had for many years designed the costumes for stars on the Vegas nightclub circuit, but I had never been involved in an effort of such magnitude.

Even with our experience and awards behind us, we had to audition for the job by submitting sketches to producer/director Donn Arden. He needed to be reassured that we were indeed capable of designing the "Tits and Feathers" show he had in mind.

Four months went into the planning of that production. For inspiration I watched endless reruns of all my favorite musicals. I constantly reminded myself as I watched that everything about "Hallelujah" would have to be bigger, sexier and more sensational than anything L.B. Mayer had dreamed up in a lifetime of musicals.

Planning sessions completed, it was time to sketch, to sew and to fit the almost one thousand costumes for a cast of more than one hundred. I ran out of inks and paints just doing the sketches.

The cost of our part of the project, which included costumes and fittings, came to just under one million dollars. The feathers alone cost two hundred thousand dollars and had to be imported from Paris. Nobody in this country was able to supply us with the necessary quantities. Finding enough iridescent rhinestones to fill our needs proved to be an almost impossible task. Before we were through we had depleted the continent of North America's supply and there wasn't a rhinestone to be found in all of Europe.

Thousands upon thousands of yards of fabric poured into the studio from every part of the country. The jewelry alone, when un-

Mitzi and her chicken

Billie
leaving brothel

(Left and opposite) Ray Aghayan and I designed the costumes for Diana Ross in the film Lady Sings the Blues, *the life story of Billie Holiday. We needed the perfect look for Billie when she first became a prostitute in Harlem in the early 1930s, but we wanted to avoid the clichéd tight, black satin dress and red feather boa look.*

Photo courtesy of Motown Productions and Paramount Pictures

wrapped and placed side by side to be counted and inspected, covered hundreds of square feet. As if this wasn't enough to keep me busy, I continued doing the weekly Carol Burnett and Cher shows, and, just to have something to occupy my spare time, I was also designing the costumes for *Funny Lady*—all simultaneously.

Days and nights began to bleed into one another. For a solid year sleep became the exception, rather than the rule. Designing and making all the costumes was very hard work, but that wasn't the half of it. Getting the costumes on the backs of the performers turned out to be a nightmare.

Show girls were hired for "Hallelujah Hollywood" and their fittings were scheduled in Los Angeles and Las Vegas. As soon as we'd fit a costume on a member of the cast, the director would switch costumes or performers and the job would begin all over.

In the meantime, due to construction problems at the hotel, the opening had to be postponed so often that many of the original performers, all of whom were hired on six-month contracts, left before the opening of the show. That meant more replacements and more fittings. Somehow it all got done. The show is now in its fifth year and still going strong. It was a valuable experience, perhaps even a once-in-a-lifetime experience.

Work goes on. There are specials, Broadway shows, a lingerie collection and a jewelry line—all of them a part of my working week. I am also taking another look at ready-to-wear clothes, which will take me back to my earlier days in the garment business.

There have been no regrets. I have been very fortunate to be a part of the world that so intrigued me as a child. I work with spectacular talent and for that alone I am pleased. But best of all is the fact that the fun, the excitement, the challenges I found in the beginning are still there. That's important, for without that, I just might as well go back to the crabgrass or the tomato-red-and-curry-yellow dishwater.

It should be the same with you. If you are serious about a career in costume design, it doesn't matter how you start or how quickly you reach your goal. What matters is how badly you want the career and how satisfied you will be when you get what you want. Because of the road I took in getting from there to here, I can offer you some advice that might help you. But in the long run, you will find your own way, just as I did.

For what it's worth, here are a few hints which may help you advance:

> High school drama departments offer excellent opportunities for experience in all aspects of the theater. It is very helpful in your future work if you have a working knowledge of scenery and make-up and know how a director achieves the finished production.

(Opposite) Here I am with Bette Midler, Elton John, Cher and Flip Wilson on Cher's first special in 1976.

Photo courtesy of Columbia Pictures and Rasta

If you are out of school, you can still call and offer your help. If this is impossible, check around for a local theater group that might be glad to have your help. It is never too early to start absorbing as much information as you can about your chosen field.

Find a school that offers a good design program. Master the basic skills of pattern making, draping and sewing. Acquire a working knowledge of such subjects as illustration, color theory and textiles.

Involve yourself in as many projects as possible. Participate in every contest, fashion show or anything else that's offered.

If you get a chance to work at a part-time job in your field, grab it. It's a great way to earn extra money and a way to gain some important practical experience.

When you've completed your studies, the number-one item on your list of priorities is to prepare a portfolio—a record of your best work. The sketches in your book should represent your best efforts. Look them over carefully and, if necessary, rework them until you are certain there is nothing you can do to improve their appearance. Include photographs whenever possible. A beautiful sketch next to a picture of the actual garment can be very impressive, and, by adding fabric swatches, you can demonstrate your sense of color and texture.

Keep yourself and your portfolio as neat and as professional-looking as possible. This doesn't necessarily mean having to wear business suits or looking as if you are working as a bank teller, but it does mean presenting a pleasant image. Just as you would analyze and dress a character in a show based upon what he is doing, so should you present yourself in the proper light. As you should know at this point in your career, appearances mean a lot. Otherwise what would you be doing in costume design?

One pitfall for a good designer to avoid is being typed. Once you have acquired a reputation for a certain kind of look, it is difficult to persuade people that you are capable of doing other things and doing them well.

(Opposite) Observing Barbra, who is observing herself, on the set of Funny Lady.

Photos courtesy of MGM Grand Hotel, Las Vegas

Donn Arden's enormously
complicated stage show,
"Hallelujah Hollywood," at
the MGM Grand Hotel in
Las Vegas.

*With Carol Channing and her
unfailing enthusiasm.*

Therefore, it is important to make your portfolio as representative as possible without trying to be the designer for all seasons. Try to avoid the things you don't understand (for instance, don't design rock clothes if that's not your thing), but make a mental note to look into such areas at a later date.

Find a job.

Once hired don't be afraid to say yes to any design challenge. If it's an area with which you are not familiar, find out what you need to know.

When you have gained as much experience as you can where you are, move onward and upward. It is too easy to become caught in the trap of security and never attempt to challenge the big leagues. The decision of where to go next depends, of course, on what you are after. If it's film, nightclub work, theater or television, you will have to go to where the action is.

Be patient. Be persistent. Be polite.

Be ready when Lady Luck knocks on your door. Being at the right place at the right time can make a big difference, but if you're not prepared, it will make no difference at all.

Be prepared to fight your own battles in the beginning; others won't do it for you. Agents are interested in people who are already successful.

When your experience warrants it, prepare a resume. Be specific. Put down everything you've done and what your related experiences are, but don't list individually all the high school plays you've worked on. Drop off your resumes in person. Mailing them won't help much.

Never leave your sketches. Give people all the time they need to look at your work, but when you are ready to leave, take your portfolio with you.

If, in spite of your precautions, someone steals one of your designs, let them. If you're good enough to be copied, you should have no problem coming up with something new.

See as many people as you can, but be realistic about your chances. Top directors and producers aren't overly enthusiastic about entrusting million-dollar projects to some starry-eyed beginner. If you are given a chance to try out for some fabulous project, however, give it all you've got. You never know when something you do will kindle a spark. When I was fresh out of school, preparations were underway to produce the stage version of *Funny Girl* on Broadway. An acquaintance, related by marriage to some member of the production staff, offered to show my sketches to the producer. I plunged into the project and gave it everything I had. Needless to say, my sketches ended up gracing the walls of some rehearsal hall. I imagined how amused the professionals must have been. I could hear them laughing at the audacity of this young kid who thought he was ready for the big time. I was disappointed, but determined not to let it throw me. Years later, Ray and I were asked to design the costumes for the sequel, *Funny Lady*. Ironically enough, it starred Barbra Streisand, whose fame had been achieved in the original *Funny Girl*.

Never be afraid to design something on speculation. You have little to lose and your gamble might pay off.

Once you have worked for a while, you might consider joining the union. In New York City you cannot design for the Broadway stage until you are a union member. This requires passing a designer's test, an extremely difficult procedure involving a four-week home project, as well as a full-day's practical examination. Very few people manage to pass this test, so the field is not crowded. In Hollywood there is the Costume Designers' Guild, and, while there is no law that says you must belong, most studios have contracts with the guild and won't employ nonmembers. It pays to join, but not until you have a job.

These twenty points can be a help to you. There are other points, also, I might mention. These are points that are true of any chosen career where the road to the top is steep, but the rewards are great. One is that you should always leave your personal problems at home when you go for an interview. Don't complain all the time when you do land a job, and, above all, don't be discouraged. If you really have what it takes, sooner or later people will begin to notice your work and recognize your name. Then you will get offers from all kinds of clients.

In the end the only thing that matters is that you hang in there and make each succeeding job better than the one before. That, I think, is the greatest challenge of all.

(Opposite) Caught in the act with Bernadette Peters.

CHAPTER TWO

A Week in the Life of a Life of a Costume Designer

Photo by Mel Fizdale

The very nature of my business makes it almost impossible to describe a typical work week, but I will choose a week when I was working on some of the last Carol Burnett Shows. It very nearly is a typical week, for even today, my routine is basically very similar, except that instead of working on that one Carol Burnett show, I'm working on a variety of shows. It's still the same sort of chaotic schedule. And my week is, if anything, even more unpredictable. Perhaps this lack of predictability is what attracts so many people to television and the other areas of show business. I seem to thrive on it.

FRIDAY

Since a great deal of my work culminates with the Friday taping of the show, it may be considered the first day of a Bob Mackie week.

Mornings are the most hectic of all. That's when some of the production numbers of each week's show are pretaped. Most of the show is taped before a live audience, but due to their size and complexity, a few numbers must be done in advance.

For me, this is the most difficult period in the week. There is no dress rehearsal, no time to check out the clothes on camera before the taping. Even with the most meticulous planning, there is the ever present risk that something might happen which will require instant attention.

Once the morning is over, those parts of the show that will be taped later before a live audience are rehearsed. This rehearsal gives me an opportunity to see the costumes in action and to make any needed last minute changes.

Today, I am sitting in the darkened theater watching the members of the cast go through their paces on stage, when the script for next week's show arrives. Its arrival marks one of the few predictable moments in my life. A new script has made its appearance at about the same time for the past eleven years.

I look at my watch. It is already 1:15 in the afternoon and the first taping before a live audience is only three hours away. I need all the time I can get to study next week's script and find out what is in store for me. I look for the dance and production numbers first, because they require the greatest amount of planning and coordination with the other members of the staff. I try to put my ideas down on paper as quickly as possible so that the fabric can be purchased and the costumes put into the works.

Few people are aware that on a weekly show such as this, the script arrives on a Friday, and, by Tuesday of the following week, we are having our first fittings. There is no time to play around. Quick decisions are a must. Dance numbers are especially difficult. Not only must the clothes fit the time period and style of the piece, but they have to be flexible, easy to move in, durable and comfortable. This is no easy task when all you have time for is one fitting.

Once I am familiar with the requirements of the production numbers, I check out the comedy sketches. The first thing I look for are the stock characters that Carol will play—Eunice, the Fat Lady, etc.—to make sure there are no changes. Eunice usually wears the same basic costume—the print dress—every time she appears, but occasionally the script calls for a change of pace.

New comedy sketches are something else entirely. To create costumes that are believable I have to know the characters I am going to dress. I have to understand the image they are supposed to project. It would be a great advantage to be able to sit down with the actors beforehand and discuss the parts each one will play, but the timing on a weekly show does not allow for such luxuries. In fact, there are times when I must decide what a character will look like before the performer has a chance to read the script. Sometimes the visual image I create will trigger new ideas in the actor's mind. This results in an entirely new characterization.

When there is time, I do ask questions to make sure I'm on the right track. With Carol it's a team effort. We pool and share our ideas.

From the script comes a great deal of inspiration—usually. This differs according to the writer. Some writers think visually. They are able to project an instant image of their characters. Others write dialog and let the creativity of the actor and the designer take over.

As I read, I make small rough sketches in the margins. These are done strictly for my benefit. I must confess, however, that there have been times when some of those thumbnail sketches have found their way into the workroom. Members of my staff have managed to magically create costumes from such scribblings.

(Opposite) Harvey Korman with Carol Burnett as the ever-lovely Stella Toddler.

(Above) Lyle Waggoner, Debbie Reynolds, Harvey Korman, Carol, John Davidson and Vicki Lawrence in a cockney number. (Left) Carol and Joel Grey as Punch and Judy. (Opposite) Liza Minnelli joined Carol in a circus finale.

Two little adorable darlings, Carol and Cher.

For the more complex costumes, I jot down notes as I read to be followed later by detailed sketches.

Once I finish the script, I look around for Ernie Flatt, the choreographer, and Paul Barnes, the set designer. They, too, will have ideas about the way a number will look. At times, I have offered suggestions that have given them an entirely new outlook. Either way, from them to me or vice versa, teamwork is important. There is, unfortunately, no time for lengthy meetings as there is in most other businesses.

The choreographer and I finish our discussion just as the stage manager announces the late lunch break. For me, it's time to get back to the office. I have to check on the progress of some twenty costumes we are making for an upcoming Mitzi Gaynor special. The office is known officially as Elizabeth Courtney Costumes. It is where all the costumes are made and fitted.

(The history behind the Elizabeth Courtney name is interesting.

When my partner, Ray, and I began working for "The Judy Garland Show," we were fortunate enough to meet and work with Elizabeth, a warm and talented lady. At that time, she was the best in her field. She excelled in the intricacies of fitting garments and had the gift of translating our sketches into the best possible finished garments. The ease with which we worked together led us eventually to invite her to join us in opening a costume house of our own. Ray and I were convinced Elizabeth was our lucky charm, so we named the house after her. She died in 1974, but her influence and name will always be with us.)

Meanwhile, back at the office, I take advantage of the break to check on the fabrics needed for next week's show. If they are not on hand, they will have to be purchased. As I arrive, the phones are ringing and a pile of messages is waiting for me on top of the counter in

Carol and Harvey Korman: a brilliant combination for ten years.

Photo courtesy of CBS

the reception area. My executive secretary, Margie Plecher, is an expert at organizing my work day and deciding which messages are priorities and how much attention they should receive. But first I run upstairs with some of the Burnett costumes. During the rehearsal I decided that some of them needed adjusting, and this is the only time the adjustments can be made. It is top priority.

As a rule, these last-minute changes are minor, but there have been times when entire costumes had to be altered or remade in time for the afternoon taping. This is a nerve-wracking process, but one we've learned to live with. While I'm upstairs, several fitters have questions about their work. Andy is making a jacket for Cheryl Ladd and wants to know how wide the lapels should be. Paulette shows me a muslin pattern for a suede skirt and asks me to mark the irregular hem I have designed. With the questions out of the way, it's back to the office to return some of the most urgent calls.

Bette Midler has phoned and would like to add a dress to her new act. Ann-Margret would like me to attend a photo session, but the session conflicts with the fittings for the Mitzi Gaynor special. While Margie juggles the day and manages to accommodate everyone (I'm never quite sure just where I'm going to be and when), the phone rings. Bernadette Peters requests a forty-foot feather boa in time for her rehearsal. Can we oblige? Of course! Every designer should be able to supply forty-foot feather boas when needed!

(Opposite and below) Carol, Ken Berry and the Ernie Flatt Dancers in a Hawaiian Sonja Henie extravaganza.

Photo courtesy of CBS

(Above) Tim Conway and Vicki Lawrence as Mr. and Mrs. Tudball. (Opposite) Dick Van Dyke and Carol in a Shirley Temple spoof.

Back upstairs, I make a final round to find out if there are any last-minute questions, when I'm paged. I pick up the receiver. It is Carol Burnett with the news that an impromptu number has just been added to the show. Will I please bring matching beaded dresses for her and Vicki Lawrence? Why not? I run back downstairs to rummage through a closet containing a number of beaded gowns that have been saved for just such emergencies. I select two I think will work and take them back to the studio with me.

And that was the lunch break.

It is 4:00 when I arrive back at Television City. The audience for the first taping has arrived and everyone is busy with last-minute adjustments while waiting for the show to begin. "The Carol Burnett

Photo courtesy of CBS

One of Carol's frequent and favorite guests, Steve Lawrence.

Show" is taped twice, each time before a different audience. One taping is at 4:15 and the other at 7:30 P.M. This gives us an opportunity to make changes when something doesn't work, and we have an alternate tape just in case a major problem develops.

As I pass the dancers on my way to Carol's dressing room, I give them a brief once-over, knowing that I will have a little time later on to check and make sure all is well. I check Carol's opening dress. She looks great. She leaves her dressing room, walks on stage and is greeted by a spontaneous ovation from her assembled fans. Carol begins her usual twenty minutes of questions and answers with the audience and I watch from the wings. Even after eleven years it is fun to watch her converse with the audience. While I am watching, Joe Hamilton, producer of the show, approaches to tell me something about next week's show.

Costume designing for T.V. is a job where you never get to

savor the end product. The minute one job is finished, it's time to start another. There is no time to just sit back and enjoy. Joe also tells me that Dave Powers, the director, would like to see me in the booth to ask a few questions about Carol's finale dress.

And the routine goes on.

After her twenty minutes with the audience, Carol returns to her dressing room to make one of her many quick changes. I say quick, because Carol is so concerned about not keeping the audience waiting that she is often ready long before the scenery is changed. While Carol is slipping into a new outfit, I check on the dancers to make sure they are ready for their number. This may be the first chance I have had to see them completely dressed with make-up and hair in place.

The minute a number is finished I take stock to make sure nothing has been torn or broken. All necessary repairs must be made during the hour between tapings. This is why I never leave the stage during a performance. Keeping a watchful eye on things is part of my job.

By 6:00 the first taping is over. My assistant and I talk over the needed repairs, if any, before I go upstairs to scrutinize the wardrobe area for costumes I may be able to use for next week's show. Needless to say, after eleven years, we've built up a sizable inventory. Though there are many times when we have to create a costume from scratch, there are other times when existing costumes can be recycled. This not only helps balance the budget, but it gives us extra time to concentrate our efforts on something special we are planning. Nothing is ever thrown away. You never know when you may have another use for that man-eating-plant costume.

I pick two dresses, a feather collar and some ruffles and hope that I can assemble them into a new costume for the following week. By now it's 7:15 and I've got to get back downstairs to check Carol for the second questions-and-answers opening. It's usually 9:00 before I am able to head home for dinner and some much needed rest.

SATURDAY

My schedule is hectic, and, when it comes to weekends, you win some and you lose some. This particular weekend, like so many others before, has fallen by the wayside. Saturday is spent at the office. There is the fitting with Mitzi, a planning session with Cher to discuss her upcoming special and I have to find time to go to International Silks and Woolens to buy fabrics for next week's Burnett Show. I often shop for fabric before completing my sketches, for there is nothing more frustrating than designing a wonderful gown only to discover the fabric needed is not available and there is no time to order it.

(Above) Leaving home Monday morning at the break of dawn! *(Above right)* Explaining a new gown for Carol to cutter and fitter, Annie Shapiro. *(Below right)* With Ed Johnson and Annette Gagnon, my wardrobe master and mistress, discussing the script.

(Above) Home at last! A snack, the paper and the late-night news. (Below) A quick meeting with wig genius, Roselle Friedland, and my assistant, Jef Billings.

Photo by Mel Fizdale

SUNDAY

Like Saturday, Sunday can turn out to be another working day, but it does have its compensations. I work at home, instead of at the office. I do my sketching in my favorite place—on top of my bed—listening to music, instead of ringing telephones and humming sewing machines. With a bit of luck, I might also manage an afternoon movie.

It's important for me to be aware of what's current and to see as many films, TV shows, etc., as possible. This is especially true with the Burnett Show, for we do so many takeoffs on current movies and fads. But this Sunday is too busy and the movie gets lost in the shuffle. Most of the day is spent working on preliminary sketches for Cher.

MONDAY

It's business as usual, if indeed there is such a thing as usual. At 7:45 A.M. I leave home for the office in order to arrive in time for the Monday meeting of my staff. We will begin official work on the Burnett Show for that week. Each person who works with me has now read the script and is armed with questions concerning his respective assignments. Annette Gagnon, who has been with me since the very first season, is responsible for all the women's clothing in general and for Carol's wardrobe in particular. Ed Johnson heads the wardrobe for the men. He is a past master at making old things look new and new things look old. He is also an expert at finding duplicate outfits for Tim Conway, whose clothes are frequently ruined during some of the messy comedy sketches. Jef Billings, my assistant, takes notes on things that need to be done and follows up on them as the week progresses. Nothing is left to chance, because when frantic Friday rolls around there is no time for changes or corrections. Sometime during the meeting, choreographer Ernie Flatt stops by to pick up Xerox copies of the costume sketches for his dancers and Roselle Friedland is on hand to check drawings of the wigs and hairstyles that I have sketched for her on a separate sheet. By 9:00, everyone is ready to tackle his respective job. I go upstairs to put the costumes into the works and to meet with Tommie and Trudy, our milliners, who are responsible for making the elaborate head-dresses that I have designed for the dancers.

The rest of the day is spent overseeing the creation of the costumes, selecting fabrics and rummaging through boxes filled with lace, appliques and jewelry.

(Opposite) Fitter Paulette Karnos and I are fitting Bernadette Peters in a 1920's dressing gown.

TUESDAY

Today is the first day of fittings. I arrive at the office at 8:00 A.M. To keep confusion at a minimum we stagger our fittings over two days—the girls on one day, the boys on another and the principals somewhere in between, depending on their individual schedules.

Tuesday is the girls' turn, and some of them have already arrived when I reach the fitting room. By 8:30 they are all milling about in various stages of undress, waiting their turn with the fitter, Elizabeth Fernandez, who makes the necessary alterations.

By 9:30 it's all over. The costumes are back upstairs, and I grab a

Carol as Maria Montez and Lyle Waggoner as the Genie.

Photo courtesy of CBS

(Above) Carol and the chorus cuties in a Busby Berkeley takeoff.
(Below) Nanette Fabray, Bonnie Evans, Carol and Harvey Korman in a 17th-century comedy epic.

package of fabric to take to the beaders in Hollywood. The heavily beaded dress is one Carol will wear in the opening of next week's show.

Beading is an intricate process involving the hand application of bugle beads, sequins and rhinestones to fragile pieces of fabric. It is an ancient art that has been handed down from generation to generation, and only a handful of people possess the skill or the willingness to tackle this time-consuming craft. When the present beaders are gone. I hope there will be someone to take their places.

The beaders' workroom is lined with shelves containing hundreds of jars and boxes filled with bits of glass twinkles from which I must select the beads and stones to decorate Carol's dress. We go over the sketches and look at the muslin pattern on which I have outlined the design I need. The timing is discussed. I explain the dress has to be ready for a fitting by the following Wednesday.

(Opposite) Carol and Bing Crosby in a turn-of-the-century melodrama. (Below) Carol and Lucille Ball.

A Week in the Life of a Costume Designer 65

Photo courtesy of CBS

The remainder of the day is spent rushing between the workroom, the drawing board and the fitting room. If all goes well, there may be time for a quick trip to the gym so that I might work off some of those snacks I have been grabbing throughout the week.

WEDNESDAY

The boys arrive for their early morning fittings. No sooner have they left when Carol Burnett arrives, early as usual. In all the years we have worked together I have never known her to be late for an appointment or a fitting. She is a consummate professional who is a delight to work with. Today she has several stories about her weekend to share with us. Annie Shapiro fits Carol in a beaded gown and a silk pants outfit. When Annie is through, Lydia comes down to fit Carol in the leotard that she will wear in the finale.

All the garments are finished on time thanks to Johnny, who runs the workroom efficiently and with incredible organization. It is Johnny who keeps everyone busy and who is responsible for meeting

(Opposite above) Carol, Eydie Gorme and Joan Rivers as the Supremes. (Opposite below) Carol and Ruth Buzzi kick up a storm with the ladies of the ensemble. (Above) Carol's yearly good-luck charm, Jim Nabors.

A Week in the Life of a Costume Designer 67

Carol: something for everyone!

the perpetual deadlines.

As Carol leaves for rehearsal, Vicki Lawrence arrives for her fittings. She will be followed by this week's guest star, Bernadette Peters.

By mid-afternoon, the fittings are over. The clothes are back in the workroom and it's time for me to drive to the studio for the weekly run-through rehearsals. It is important for me to be there because many needs that may not be evident in the script will become obvious in the run-through.

On this particular day I find that Carol is planning to spill glue all over Tim Conway, which means I have to make arrangements for an

extra set of clothes, just in case they are needed. It is the only time during the week when all members of the Burnett staff get together for a chance to review each others' progress. The run-through takes place in a large, barren rehearsal hall, one of the many at Television City. Its dismal atmosphere in no way hampers anyone's spirits. The assembled actors go through their paces as though they were performing for an actual audience. Aside from an occasional inside joke, the proceedings—like everything else connected with the Burnett show—is businesslike and professional. At the conclusion of the run-through, my assistants and I discuss any problems that might need solving before I return to the shop for yet another fitting.

Roddy McDowall and Ken Berry join Vicki Lawrence and Carol in a musical tribute to Fred Astaire and Ginger Rogers.

A Week in the Life of a Costume Designer 71

THURSDAY

The morning is spent putting the finishing touches on costumes. While I'm busy assembling Carol's jewelry and a fur piece for her opening sketch, I learn that one of the planned numbers has been dropped and another substituted. Fortunately for me, the new sketch involves one of Carol's stock characters and there are no last-minute problems. At 11:30 I am told that Cher is at CBS rehearsing her special. I track her down so that we can discuss some of my designs for her show. We manage a few minutes together, during which she tells me she wants to play all six male characters from the musical *West Side Story*. Dressing Cher does not always require pretty dresses.

The minute our meeting is over I have to travel to NBC, which is across town, where Mitzi is scheduled to begin her first day of taping.

Later in the evening I meet Cher for a photo session at Harry Langdon's studio. It's 1:30 in the morning when I get home.

FRIDAY

The week has come full circle. Another Friday has arrived, and, by 9:00 A.M. I'm in the make-up department at CBS to scrutinize the dancers who are preparing for another of those pretaped numbers.

Promptly at 1:15 the script for next week's show arrives. It is heavier than its predecessors, containing the material for the last "Carol Burnett Show," a two-hour special. It will bring down the final curtain on eleven wonderful and exciting years—one more poignant reminder that a very special chapter in my life is about to come to an end. Automatically, as I have done so many times before, I open the script and glance at the pages, looking for dance numbers and comedy sketches. But all that seems to surface is nostalgia.

As I look around for Ernie or Paul, I realize that each one of us will be affected differently by Carol's decision to close the show. I'll continue my work, remembering what Carol has said to me on many occasions, "change is growth." But I know that something special will be missing from my life. The family I have worked with for eleven years can never be replaced. But, as I look at my watch, I realize that now is not the time to think about those things. It is 2:15 and the run-through is about over. I must return to the shop to answer messages, select fabric and begin another week. This time I will be preparing for the last "Carol Burnett Show."

(Opposite) Carol on the last show.

PART TWO:

A More Glamourous You

The concept of glamour has fascinated and intrigued us for centuries. Thousands of pictures and stories about glamourous people have been printed in magazines and newspapers. TV shows and movies have capitalized on images of glamour and "the beautiful people."

An individual's glamour is as distinctive as the personality itself. We can speak of pubescent glamour, sports glamour, political glamour and the glamour of movie stars. Sometimes people are glamourous because of what they do, what they have done or how well they do it. Glamour comes from an incredible personality, a charisma that draws and warms an audience in a special way. It can also come from the fact that a person photographs well; some stars are glamourous only on film. There is religious glamour—the Pope certainly has that—and there is the glamour of power and money. Great intellect has its own appeal; Einstein was no beauty, but he was certainly glamourous. Some—as the old saying goes—are born with it, others achieve it and others have it thrust upon them.

Perhaps the concept is too illusionary to be pinned down with a concrete definition, but I do believe that all of us, you and I included, have the sparks of glamour. And we can enhance what we have. Perhaps this book will enable you to bring your unique glamour into its own, for glamour is certainly, in part, a physical attractiveness. It is not just a beaded gown or a gorgeous hairdo, not simply a beautiful face and a fabulous figure; but it is a physical appeal that is pleasing. It is that mysterious magic of which stars are made. We all know it when we see it. You have seen it among your friends and acquaintances. You are at a party, people are sitting around talking, and then the door opens and a woman steps into a room. Instantly, the conversa-

Photo courtesy of ABC

UPI

UPI

(Opposite) The Kennedys: political glamour.
(Above left) Donny and Marie: pubescent
glamour. (Below left) Pope John Paul: religious
glamour. (Above right) Muhammad Ali: sports
glamour.

Shirley Temple

Fred Astaire

tion lulls as all eyes move to the new arrival. There is something about her presence that captures the imagination. No one may be able to say exactly what it is, but everyone knows it is there.

It's the sort of thing that happens when a superstar walks onto a stage or in front of a camera. The Hollywood star system is one of the most obvious examples of how important glamour can be. Why is it that some very attractive, very talented performers never reach the superstar status that others have? It is, undoubtedly, due to that remarkable quality we call glamour.

The interior image we have of ourselves is what counts the most, and, if the qualities of confidence and self-control are there to begin with, it is difficult to cover them up.

There are numerous ways to enhance glamour. Make-up, judiciously applied, the right clothes worn well and a complementary hairdo can go a long way toward achieving a glamourous image. A dull, rather average-looking person can be turned into a fascinating creature, capable of mesmerizing millions, simply through the use of exterior ornamentation and the ability to appear totally relaxed and self-assured. Glamourous people may not be as confident as they seem in all situations, but they certainly present an assured exterior.

They smile easily and their personalities radiate confidence.

A good designer can make almost anyone appear glamourous at first sight. But the depth of that glamour depends on the person's own attitudes and actions. A loud, unpleasant personality can effectively defeat the most stunning wardrobe. Glamour is a partnership between good grooming and gracious behavior.

Glamour, of course, is very much a part of my life, since my career revolves around the performing arts. A big part of my job as a designer is to enhance and improve what these glamourous people already have. I don't remake clients, but I do emphasize their strong points and minimize their weak ones. I show them off to their best advantage. It is something you should do for yourself. And with a few hints from me, I'm sure you'll be able to.

glamourous Job!

CHAPTER THREE

Mirror, Mirror

With the arrival of each new season, ever-increasing numbers of fashion experts hand out various kinds of conflicting advice on how to dress and what to look for in order to be in "style."

The question of what to wear is becoming increasingly difficult to answer. There are no hard-and-fast rules to go by. New Yorkers don't dress as Californians do. What is right in Dallas is probably wrong in Chicago. And that is only the beginning. Your wardrobe requirements are based on a number of factors that include not only where you live and the standards of your community, but on *how* you live and *what* you do.

Dressing well is a difficult problem. But in order to solve such a complicated puzzle in the most efficient manner, it is best to start with the basics.

BUILDING A BASIC WARDROBE

I hardly need remind you of what has been happening to the price of clothes, and, as if the rising costs weren't bad enough, each price hike appears to be accompanied by a drop in the quality and workmanship of the clothing. As a result, a good wardrobe has become a rather costly investment. Its selection deserves the same thought and care as the purchase of any other long-lasting necessity.

A basic wardrobe consists of affordable clothes that suit both your personality and your life-style. There is no such thing as a basic wardrobe for everyone. The needs of an airline hostess differ from those of a secretary. A corporation president's wardrobe would not be the same as that of a television performer. A housewife selects different clothes than does a courtroom lawyer. Regardless of the life-style, however, every woman is better off with a limited selection of well-made, classic clothes than she is with a closet full of odds and ends. The classics will look as good next year as they do right now.

Cleaning Out the Deadwood

Before beginning your new wardrobe, there is something you should do first. Go through your closet and evaluate everything you own. Keep anything that is really usable, but eliminate the deadwood—those little numbers you haven't worn in years, but just haven't got the heart to throw away. Chances are they will never again see the light of day or night, so you may as well get rid of them. They do take up space.

Once you've made some room and have a fairly good idea of what you have to build on, it's time to start adding one piece at a time until you have created the kind of wardrobe that includes all the important essentials.

The First Major Purchases

Let's say you are ready to begin shopping. Your first major purchase will be a pair of fall or winter slacks. Why not get some that are fully lined and made from good-quality wool? The price may be a bit steeper than you are used to paying, but you'll find the appearance, fit and wearability of the pants will more than make up for the extra cost.

If a blazer or skirt is next on your list, make sure each matches something you already have. Too many women fall into the same trap year after year. They buy so many unrelated items that they end up without a single complete outfit by the time the season is over. If that has happened to you, there can be only one or two reasons why: Either you have money to burn or you are the victim of your own poor planning.

Should You Follow the Fashion?

Fashion *is* important, but I do not suggest you rid yourself of everything you own every time a new trend begins.

Let's assume you look great in a pair of slacks and blazer, but the current trend calls for skirts and sweaters. You can continue to wear the pants and blazer, by all means. The only time you should update your look is when it is no longer fresh-looking on you or when you have become bored with it. In that case, replace it with something else, something new.

Trendy items are fleeting in public popularity, and nothing looks more dated than yesterday's fads. But don't hold yourself too firmly in check. If the current fashion passion is oversized jackets with padded shoulders and everyone except you has already dashed out to buy a couple and you are just dying to have one, go! Indulge yourself. But do so with care. Select a style that is not too extreme, unless you are

prepared to donate your purchase to Goodwill at the end of the season.

Above all, don't attempt to keep up with the trendsetters, *unless* you have both the inclination and the cash. There will always be women with the time and the money and the desire to dress in the latest style. They are fully prepared to give up their wardrobe at the end of the season and start another. But it is a game that few women can afford to play.

Color-Coordinated Separates

All in all, it takes surprisingly little to put together a workable, basic wardrobe. Listed below are some examples of pieces to look for and suggestions on how to wear them.

You will find that the basics on my list consist of separates—exclusively. This is because separates are easier to coordinate and will go further in stretching a limited clothes budget.

The best way to start is by selecting one or two basic color schemes that work well for you and sticking to them. Let's assume you own a navy blue skirted suit. To it you might add a grey skirt, a pair of grey pants, a red blazer, and a navy or grey cardigan. Each will mix and match. Complete the look by adding two tailored blouses, one in red and the other in white, a grey V-neck pullover, with long sleeves, to be worn either over a blouse or with a scarf and some jewelry and a navy turtleneck that can be worn alone or topped by a shirt. In addition, you will need one pair of navy and one pair of grey shoes. One is for walking and the other should have heels. Last, but by no means least, you should purchase a smartly styled, well-made leather bag to go with everything you own.

You will now have the following:
- a navy blue skirted suit
- a grey skirt
- a pair of grey slacks
- a red blazer
- a navy (or grey) cardigan
- two tailored blouses (red and white)
- a grey V-neck pullover
- a navy turtleneck
- two pairs of shoes (navy and grey, low- and high-heeled)
- a leather purse to go with everything

The shoes are very important. Having spent time and money on a good wardrobe, don't ruin the effect with those old, tired-looking shoes you have been wearing for years. Nothing will spoil a look faster than poorly coordinated or worn out accessories.

The same basic principles will work with other color combinations, including beige, rust and brown; ivory, black and light blue; or with other neutrals that coordinate well.

The reason I recommend solids, rather than prints and patterns, is that they are easier to work with and you can always alter their appearance with a contrasting accessory. Also, people tend to remember prints more readily. Therefore, you would need to have a sizable wardrobe in order to make prints and patterns a good investment. The same rule applies to coats. If one is all you can afford, find one that will go with everything in your closet. A classic raincoat in a conservative shade with a zip-out lining will make an excellent cover-up for lots of occasions. In a colder climate get yourself a good wool wraparound in a neutral color, heavy enough to keep you warm and long enough to cover your hemlines.

WHEN THE SUN GOES DOWN

There are as many ways of dressing for an evening out as there are evenings to dress for. Nights out can range from a romantic dinner for two by candlelight to a neighborhood backyard barbecue. You might be attending a reception at the boss' home or dining out at your favorite restaurant with friends. Each event calls for a different look, yet they all have one thing in common—you. Unlike some fictional characters, people don't change their style or personality with the setting of the sun. A chic, tailored daytime woman can't turn herself into a Scarlett O'Hara by moonlight. It simply doesn't work.

I am constantly amazed by the number of women who look absolutely stunning from nine to five and then proceed to turn themselves into a total disaster for the evening. Not knowing what to wear at night seems to be a dilemma shared by many. In all fairness I must admit it is easier to find the right thing to wear to a business meeting than it is to a dinner party.

To add to the confusion invitations can be misleading. The invitation might specify white-tie, black-tie, black-tie optional, semiformal, informal or casual, and it may mean exactly that; and again, it may not.

If the invitation says *black-tie* and it means what it says, the affair will be a formal one, with the men in tuxedos or dinner jackets and the ladies in formal evening attire (not necessarily floor length, but more about that later).

Black-tie optional or *semiformal* calls for dressy dinner dresses or suits and a dark suit and tie for men.

Informal means a simple attractive dress or smart-looking sportswear for women, and for men, slacks and a sportscoat.

Casual could mean anything, depending on the event and the location. To me it means denims or jeans, a T-shirt and a pair of tennis shoes.

That's also what it meant to Carol Burnett when she received an invitation that said to dress "beachy." When she arrived at her destination, she was amazed and more than a little embarrassed to find her hostess and everyone else in their Sunday finery. She was

Formal—Black Tie

dressed in jeans, a T-shirt and sandals. The moral of the story is that, unless you know your hostess and host and their way of doing things, it might be a good idea to call ahead and find out specifically what you should wear.

Semi Formal

Casual

The Glamourous Hostess

If you are the one who is doing the entertaining, what you wear will depend on your guest list and the type of occasion. If you're planning a seductive evening for two by candlelight, it might be worth your while to learn something about your guest before setting the scene. A sexy, informal sort of gown that molds to your body and reveals a great deal of your charms may encourage your guest to shed his coat and tie and enter into the spirit of things. But this is a scenario that doesn't work with everyone. The man who parks his Honda at the curb and arrives in jeans, expecting a cold beer and a casual meal, may well be put off by your jersey dress and the crystal goblets.

One of the nicest things about being hostess is that exotic or unusual clothes, which may be totally out of place on the street or at the theater, may be perfect for entertaining at home. That multicolored caftan or the authentic, handwoven skirt, which you may have picked up in your travels and which will look wonderful worn with a long-sleeved turtleneck sweater, could be just the right touch for your evening. Another glamourous way for the hostess to dress is in ankle- or floor-length skirts with elegant satin or silk shirts. Sexy hostess pajamas also can be nice.

Dressing for your guests is a very personal way of letting them know how much their company means to you.

The Dress for That One Special Occasion

Unless you have a lot of money to spread around, don't waste it on evening clothes. It makes absolutely no sense to blow a small fortune on some little dress you plan to wear only once or twice. If you are faced with having to buy a long dress, pick a style that will enable you to cut off the length once it has served its purpose. That way you can at least continue to wear the dress on less formal occasions.

There are other solutions for what to wear on a formal occasion if you don't want to buy an evening gown. Whatever the event, you are always safe in a short, understated dinner dress made from jersey, crepe or some other such fabric. Another excellent solution is a good black suit. After a day at the office, you can transform the black suit into something quite glamourous simply by changing to a dressy blouse and adding some gold chains or a string of pearls.

Solving the Wrap Problem

The added advantage to wearing suits is that they answer that nagging business of what to do about a wrap, a problem that stumps most women (including some of my clients).

If you live in a cold climate and have a very busy social schedule, a long coat or cape can be a dramatic way to cover up an evening dress. But not all of you want to invest that kind of money, especially

At Home Entertaining

since a wrap is the one thing you shed the moment you arrive at your destination. I see nothing wrong with wearing your regular winter coat over a short dinner dress. If you are wearing a long dress and cannot afford a long wrap, wear a shorter coat and remove it just before arriving at your destination.

In warmer weather all you need is something to protect your arms and shoulders. A large square that can be folded and tied or a short jacket made from a soft, rich-looking fabric will do quite nicely.

Overdressing

One of the worst offenses of all is overdressing. This happens when women are unsure of what to wear at a particular function or place. I have witnessed it many times, especially in such places as restaurants that have suddenly become very popular and have been written up in the gossip and society columns as the "in" places to visit. Once that type of publicity gets around, some women will begin showing up for dinner looking totally out of place. They will be wearing long, elaborate dinner gowns. Chances are the restaurant owes its newly found popularity to an understated, subdued ambiance (not counting the food and service), which calls for simple dinner dresses or dressy suits, rather than showy evening clothes.

Whether you are planning to spend the evening at the boss' house or visiting the newest night spot in town, play it down by dressing on the conservative side, especially if you don't know what to expect. An understated dress with a nice high neck and long sleeves can be far more dramatic and effective than some low-cut, flamboyant number that leaves little to the imagination.

After-five looks don't have to be conservative, of course. Lots of festive occasions are the perfect settings for glamourous fabrics, vibrant colors and jewelry that glitters by candlelight. But it is a good idea to find out something about the occasion and the setting before deciding on what to wear.

Shopping for Evening Wear

While you are looking for some after-five fashions, give some consideration to what a dress will look like at the end of a long evening after hours on the dance floor. You need to find something that is comfortable, that fits well and that won't embarrass you by slipping its moorings halfway through the night.

If you have the sort of active social life that requires a variety of evening clothes and you don't have a lot of money to spend, try treating your nighttime wardrobe as you would the daytime version. Buy things that match and stick to one or two color schemes. That way you won't need a different pair of shoes for each outfit, and one or two evening bags will match everything you own.

Overdressed ?

Except for large formal events or entertaining at home, floor-length evening dresses are a poor investment. They are difficult to drive in, get soggy in rain or snow, and they are hopeless when flagging down taxicabs. Hemlines ranging anywhere from just below the knees to just above the ankles, depending on the social occasion, not only look good, but are more in tune with the times.

A SPECIAL DATE

Wherever you happen to be heading on your special date, and I believe all dates should be special, a man wants to be proud of the way you look when he takes you out. The best thing you can do for his ego and yours is to look gorgeous. He will be the envy of every other man around. (Of course, he owes you the same favor.)

Convert a long, formal dress into a less formal one by cutting off the excess length.

If you plan a night on the town, select clothes that are soft and easy. For dressier occasions there is nothing like silk, jersey, crepe de chine or cashmere to make you look and feel feminine and desirable. Dating clothes should be comfortable; you can't possibly have a good time in something so tight that you have to worry about each move you make.

Pick colors that will flatter your hair and skin. You may be pleasantly surprised how much sparkle and excitement this will add to your evening. Some women are absolutely stunning dressed in vibrant, exotic shades they wouldn't dream of wearing during the daytime. Bright red or kelly green may flatter one woman, while others will look wonderful in deep burgundy, emerald green or cobalt blue.

I happen to love white for night because of the marvelous things it can do to a woman's face. White also softens, if it is worn next to the face. I also like black for evenings; it is sexy and exciting by candlelight, especially if worn with touches of glittering jewelry.

A special date is the perfect time for those added little touches that let him know you think he's worth your attention. Wear that pretty dinner ring you've saved for just the right time and add an extra dab of perfume or more dramatic eye make-up.

There are other ways to make the date more festive. Treat yourself to luxurious and beautiful lingerie to wear under your outfit. A woman should feel glamourous from the skin out. Extra-sheer hose will give your legs a sleek, sexy look. Add the high-heeled evening sandals and you'll feel and be gorgeous. But, please, if you think you might be dancing, be sure you can navigate in the shoes you wear. It is no fun to dance with a partner who can barely walk, let alone dance.

You are dressed and ready to leave the house. It's time to bid farewell to that favorite oversized handbag for the evening. Not only will it spoil your overall look, but imagine how you would feel if it tipped over and spilled its contents during the course of your evening. Instead, carry a small, attractive envelope bag that holds what you need and leave the gunnysack where it belongs—at home.

Many women are convinced that the way to flatter a man is to ask his advice on what to wear. I don't agree. Most men are embarrassed by that question, some could care less and others wouldn't know how to answer if they did. If he is taking you somewhere for the very first time and you haven't a clue what to wear, ask; but be prepared for an awkward or a noncommittal answer. The best way to find out what he likes on you is to wait until he compliments you on the way you look. If he should express a dislike for something you have on and his opinion is important to you, avoid wearing it when you're together.

Regardless of whom you're trying to please—men, women or yourself—there is only one thing that should dictate the kind of clothes you wear, and that is your personality. A special mood could easily influence your style of dressing, but basically, you have an image you want to project, and the best appearances come from the extension of that image.

A special date can be many things. It can be an intimate evening for two, a visit to the neighborhood movie theater or an afternoon at the ball park. What you wear will depend on the occasion. What counts for your sake, as well as his, is to look as good as you possibly can.

DOWN THE AISLE

Unless a wedding invitation stipulates white- or black-tie, there is no need to drag out your most elegant possessions and attend the affair dressed to the hilt. Nothing is very attractive about a woman decked out in a long, formal gown being escorted by a man in a business suit. A wedding may be a show, but its only star should be the bride.

If the ceremony is informal, dressing for the event should be no different from dressing for an evening at the theater or a visit to a nice restaurant. While there is something very romantic about a garden wedding on a warm, sunny afternoon, the perfect setting for a voile dress in pastel or a soft floral print, a linen suit or any attractive summer dress from your closet would serve just as well.

For a formal affair wear a dinner suit or a street-length cocktail dress in any color but white, which should be reserved for the bride.

The Star of the Show

If you are the bride, pick a gown that is an extension of your regular taste in clothes, one that will match your personality. Because you will be so busy at the conclusion of the ceremony greeting guests, being photographed or dancing, your gown should be comfortable enough to allow you to move freely.

If you happen to be the type who looks lovely in old-fashioned lace, this is your opportunity to be that princess you've always dreamed of being. If, on the other hand, you are a suntanned, sporty type and you look as if you spend every spare minute on the beach or the ski slopes, you will be better off with a simpler, more sophisticated gown.

The Star's Mother

Being the mother of the bride doesn't mean that you have to immerse yourself in baby blue or beige lace. Neither does it mean that you have to wear a floor-length gown, unless the ceremony is a formal one. Select something that will fit (1) your personality, (2) the color of the bridal party and (3) your own freedom of movement.

This is important since you will be expected to mingle with the guests and oversee last-minute preparations.

If you normally wear clothes that are on the tailored side, adapt that look for the occasion. There are many clothes appropriate for the mother of the bride; you do not have to resort to the stereotypical lace gown with dyed-to-match shoes.

SPORTS AND THE GREAT OUTDOORS

Whether you are heading for the bleachers to watch the ball game or an afternoon picnic at the park, you can afford to go in style thanks to that triumph of the American fashion industry, spectator sportswear. No other area of ready-to-wear offers such an abundance of smart, practical, wearable clothes designed for so many tastes and occasions.

Summer is the time for being informal and comfortable in casual clothes. Outdoor sports events are the perfect setting. By being comfortable I don't mean that you should wear those favorite beat-up grubbies that are so wonderful for around the house. There is nothing that says comfort can't be chic.

Sportswear for watching—not playing—includes denims (both pants and skirts), T-shirts and other cotton tops, windbreakers, sweat shirts, sweaters or denim jackets. Jeans, an indispensable item for casual living, are suitable for all sorts of occasions.

For those who can't wait to get a headstart on a summer tan, there are abbreviated clothes that are designed for maximum exposure. These include sun dresses, tank tops and shorts.

To protect hair and face from wind and sun women can choose from an endless array of headgear, including big, floppy hats, visors, bandanas and, of course, authentic baseball caps.

No sporty look would be complete without a pair of barefoot sandals, tennis shoes, bright scarves, colorful (or white) beads, a pair of stylish sunglasses and an attractive straw or canvas bag.

Whether it's in the bleachers or the grandstand, a sporty look is the natural one. This includes keeping make-up to a minimum and wearing a simple, easy-to-care-for hairstyle.

In the Swim

Sales records may fail to bear out my theory, but I believe that ninety-nine percent of all women look better in one-piece bathing suits. Bikinis and two-piece suits look good only on very well-proportioned, well-toned bodies.

Any suit is appropriate for the privacy of your own backyard, even the skimpiest. But when you are out in public, others will be looking at you. Don't wear a bikini if it doesn't look good on you, no matter what the fashion is. An attractive one-piece suit that fits well, is comfortable, and gives needed support to the bust will always be in fashion.

If you are a sun worshipper who loves to expose as much skin as possible and your body is not what it used to be, wear a cover-up until it's time to lie down for some serious tanning.

Ideally, bathing suits should be as comfortable in the water as out, but you will probably have to shop around to find one that is equally suited for swimming and sunning. The best styles have straps that can be tied and/or buttoned in the water and then removed and tucked away while sunbathing. This will avoid those unattractive lines that spoil an otherwise beautiful, even tan.

On the Greens, on the Court or on a Yacht

As I have previously mentioned, there is an endless variety of ready-to-wear casual clothes from which to choose. Follow my advice on other aspects of your wardrobe to choose your most flattering ten-

nis, golfing or yachting outfits. What I mean is, if you are overweight (see page 142), don't wear very tight slacks on the golfing green. Wear an easy comfortable skirt with the appropriate shoes.

I do have one pet peeve. Clothing that is worn for active participation in sports is not appropriate for streetwear or to wear while sitting around sipping drinks at a party—except for the most casual. Too many women believe that their tennis outfits are suitable for any occasion. I disagree. I also believe that tennis skirts are more flattering on women than tennis shorts, but that is a matter of individual taste.

If you are invited to a yachting party for a week or a long weekend, pack your swimsuit, shorts and other casual wear that you would use at a beach party. Dresses to wear for dinner should be comfortable and attractive, but don't pack evening clothes or a cocktail dress unless specifically reminded to do so by your host.

THE EXPECTANT MOTHER

Women who can sew and make their own clothes are very fortunate when it comes to dealing with a wardrobe during the six months—more or less—when they are expecting. They can make themselves some very attractive outfits at inexpensive prices by picking up patterns that are designed for such times.

If you cannot sew, maybe you have a mother, mother-in-law or friend who can. Unless you plan to be pregnant every year for a while, it doesn't make sense to rush out and buy an entirely new wardrobe that you will wear only for a few months.

If you do choose to buy some items, select separates that can be made over after your baby has arrived or that can be worn belted (as a tunic top) without alterations.

ON THE JOB

While there has been a lot of print set describing how successful women dress for their careers, I feel I should add my voice to the roar of the crowd. I'm not saying your appearance will guarantee you a successful climb up the corporate ladder, but I am saying it will go a long way in telling people who you are and where you stand. If you dress like a loser, you are likely to be written off as such. Most winners have style, which has less to do with looks and the latest trends than it has to do with the way they carry themselves, their conversation and how they move. It is the total way they come across to others; in other words their exterior image.

The way you wear your clothes can be as important as what you wear. You need not be rich or beautiful to have style, neither do you have to be a walking fashion plate. Style is knowing how to dress in clothes that look good on you. Fashion is the current look, but clothes that are comfortable, are appropriate for what you do and are your

Outdoors

individual style may not be the latest fashion rage.

Contrary to popular belief, few designers expect you to wear a look exactly as they have created it. They are aware that you must make their clothes work for you. On the other hand, a garment that needs too much alteration may not be the right piece for you.

I do want to point out that wearing what you feel you look best in can be a trap. While feeling good about the way you look is important, you cannot lose touch completely with what is going on around you. Something that looked wonderful on you ten years ago may no longer work for you today. You may still look the same; in fact, you may not have changed much at all. But the world around you has changed, and the cut of the skirt you loved ten years ago may look totally dated today. Dated clothes will date you.

Designers are not trying to pull one over on you by regularly changing and updating their concepts. They bring out a collection each season because they have newer and fresher ideas, and—like everyone else—they want to make money. They are in business, and making money in business is being successful, which brings us back to the point—women in business.

When a woman chooses a business career, she wishes to succeed. She is working toward a positive goal. Therefore, women should dress positively for their careers. They should not attempt to be a carbon copy of their male co-workers. A woman should be feminine and stylish at all times, but she should never let her clothes overshadow what she does or says.

On the Job?

By feminine I don't mean fussy, skin-tight, revealing clothes. These are just as out of place on the job as are bracelets that clank against desk tops or rings that sparkle on every finger of each hand (a look I find very unattractive both in and out of the office). What I do mean is to create a well-put-together, business, office look by utilizing clothes that are chic, comfortable and attractive. The clothes shouldn't wrinkle easily and they should keep their shape through the day—and night, too, if necessary.

Conservative, neutral colors are, of course, more appropriate to the executive suite than are vibrant, exotic prints. On the other hand, I see nothing wrong with brightening your appearance by adding a touch of color here and there in the form of a blouse or scarf.

I'm all for women wearing a light shade next to their faces, because, as I mentioned earlier, it not only softens the face, but it tends to flatter women. It is safer to stick to soft pastels, such as light blue, peach, pale yellow and soft green. Business blouses should be tailored and made from a good fabric, such as silk, synthetics resembling silk, cottons and cotton blends.

A blouse that ties at the throat looks great topped by a V-neck sweater. A turtleneck sweater worn under a smart shirt is also nice. When worn alone, sweaters look better when they match the color of the pants or skirts. Incidentally, the pants and skirts should fit you in such a way that they won't pull or ride up each time you sit down.

When a woman enters the world of business, she is merely extending herself naturally. She should dress the same way. Her clothes should be a natural extension of her own personality.

On the Job!

CHAPTER FOUR

The Ultimate Illusion

Our age of instant communication and split-second decisions has perhaps contributed to our tendency to judge people by how they look, rather than by what they are. If so, it is only that more emphasis is placed today on what has always been true. We have always been taught that "clothes make the man," even while being admonished not to "judge a book by its cover." But we still do judge the book by the cover very often.

Our clothing does reflect our life-style. What we wear tells the world who we are at the moment, or at least who we would like to be. Those people who say they can't afford to dress well or that how they look doesn't affect their performance are kidding themselves. Performances are affected by what others think of us, and, in actuality, anyone can afford to dress well.

The biggest difference between most women and that gorgeous creature on the TV or film screen is patience, determination, time and a healthy dose of personal pride. Stars, it has been said, are made, not born, and that is especially true of the image they project. These women did not spring full blown and glittering into the world. They were not all blessed with perfect skins, perfect figures and perfect hair. They have worked with the attributes they have and have learned to cover their least attractive features, while playing up their good ones.

Beauty is a strange animal. Perfect features are seldom beautiful. It's the slight imperfections, such as a small gap between the teeth, or the crooked little smile or a dimpled chin that add style that wouldn't be there if all were perfect.

You will grant that all people are not created equal, won't you? Bodies come in various shapes and sizes. Everyone has features she would just as soon not advertise. The ultimate trick is knowing how to

play up what's good and play down what's not. That is creating an illusion, and illusion is one of the secrets of glamour.

Barbra Streisand's nose certainly caused a sensation. Before she became the superstar that she is, her type of nose was considered unattractive. Women with perfectly acceptable noses had been running out to have them bobbed. In fact, for over twenty years, plastic surgeons turned untold thousands of young women into so many look-alike Gidgets.

It is a sad commentary on a society when it is unable to see beauty in many different types of features and in women of all ages. Perhaps it is a sign of our growing maturity as a nation that we are now beginning to do so, or perhaps it is just that women of all types are beginning to package themselves more attractively, and, as the stars learn, packaging is an important aspect of looking good. Packaging is not all that simple, however. As anyone who has attempted to wrap a present knows, it takes more than a sheet of lovely paper and some pretty ribbon to do an even adequate job.

By following a few simple rules, I know you can learn how to camouflage your imperfections. A figure like Cher's may not be your asset, but there is a lot you can do with what you have, even if the shape of your fanny, the size of your feet or the contour of your waist leaves much to be desired.

The first step in the process is deciding what you want your image to be and then going after the image as best you can without losing sight of your limitations.

Gather your courage and stand before a full-length mirror in the buff. Take a good critical look at yourself. Note your assets, but also note your shortcomings.

One of the limitations many women face is the fact that they are overweight, but there are other limitations that have nothing to do with weight. Everyone has shortcomings of the body, for which no solution can be found in cottage cheese diets or in celery stalks.

There are stocky necks, short-thick waists and heavy legs. Yet all these problems can be minimized. How to cope with these problems is what I want to talk to you about in this chapter.

If you were my client, coming to see me for the first time, you would have your measurements taken by a member of my staff who is trained to record those vital statistics accurately. I would then have a chart specially prepared containing all of the information I would need in order to design clothing for you. You should do the same thing for yourself at home.

PRETTY HAIR

I have rarely met a woman who didn't have something unkind to say about her hair. The misfortunes that befall the female head seem

Barbra Streisand.

Photo courtesy of Columbia Pictures and Rastar

endless. "My hair is too curly," some women complain. "Mine is too straight," say others. Hair is too thick, too thin, dull, lifeless, it loses its body in the rain and it frizzes each time the weather is damp.

It isn't really possible to change the texture of your hair, but it is possible to do something about its color and style. Since hair serves as a frame for your face, it ought to be styled in such a manner that complements your features, as well as your complexion.

Very long hair, unless it is worn up, rarely looks good on a woman over thirty-five. (I did say rarely, for there is always that exceptional woman.)

When it comes to hair, I have one cardinal rule to follow for which I make no exceptions, however. It has nothing to do with long, short, thick, thin, straight or curly. It has to do with cleanliness. I believe that regardless of style, hair cannot look attractive unless it is clean and shiny.

There is no truth to that old wives' tale that too much washing will take the natural oils out of your hair. To keep their hair looking shiny and smelling sweet, actresses and models shampoo daily. While this may be too awesome to contemplate for some, three shampoos per week are a must if you want to keep dirt, dust and perspiration from penetrating your scalp. You should also choose your shampoos carefully. Avoid harsh detergent shampoos and stick to a low, naturally balanced pH shampoo. Ask your hairdresser to recommend a good one for your type of hair.

Though nature has its own way of softening the hair when age takes over by adding grey, many women would prefer not to let nature take its course. Not all grey is attractive, in any case. So, if you don't like what nature has dished out, cover it up. Be careful, however, in your choice of colors. Shades that are too dark will appear harsh and will add age. Unless you are a natural blonde, the color you choose to eliminate the grey should be slightly lighter and softer than your youthful color was.

FLATTERING MAKE-UP

Just as your attire should, make-up can bring out the best in you. After all, most people will look at your face before they notice the rest of you, so the right kind of make-up, properly applied, can work to your advantage.

Using make-up correctly takes practice. You should have good light and a magnifying mirror. Remember, too, that a little will go a long way. A heavy coat of make-up can be aging and unattractive. It will tend to seep into the creases and wrinkles of the skin, which will then call attention to the very thing you are trying to hide.

The right make-up should flatter your complexion and give you a youthful glow, a natural appearance. During the day, a soft, clear

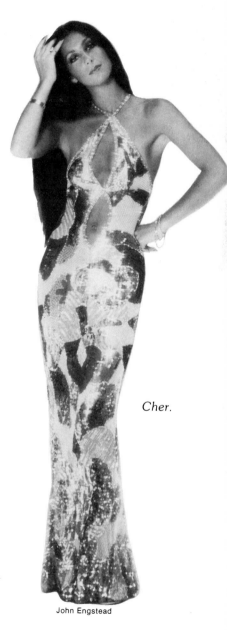

Cher.

John Engstead

foundation worn with a dash of blusher, a bit of lipstick and a touch of eye make-up is all that most women need.

At night, you can be more extreme. Dramatic eyes, an extra pair of lashes and intense shades of blusher and lipstick are far more flattering under the soft, dim lights of night than they are in the harsh glare of the sun.

MAKING THE MOST OF THE NECK

To the Japanese the nape of the neck is one of the sexiest parts of a woman's body. The geishas show off their napes by baring the upper portion of their backs and wearing their long hair up.

I do think there is nothing lovelier than a long slender neck, the kind that did so much for Audrey Hepburn. It looks great no matter what you do with it.

Do !

Figs. 1, 2, 3

Too Thick, Too Scrawny or Too Long

If your neck tends to be overly long or on the thick side, your best bet is to cover it. This covered look works well with a neck that is too scrawny also. Turtlenecks and high collars, wide chokers or ascot-tied blouses (figures 1,2 and 3) work well. Whatever you do use to cover up, make sure it is kept loose.

While shirt collars with a high stand can be flattering, pendants at the end of a long chain or V-necklines will lengthen the neck and accentuate the problem (figures 4, 5 and 6). Also, a slightly longer, fuller hairstyle is more flattering to a woman whose neck is not of the best shape (figures 1, 2 and 3).

Hiding the Age Lines

The neck also happens to be one of the first areas of the body to

Figs. 4, 5, 6

Don't !

Figs. 7, 8, 9

Do !

Figs. 10, 11, 12

reveal age. In an attempt to cover up this unwelcomed evidence, many women resort to chokers, high-standing collars (figures 7 and 8) or tightly wrapped scarves. This may cause others to wonder at what terrible secrets are lurking beneath all that camouflage. These things also tend to emphasize the problem by catching in the folds of skin and drawing attention to the problem they are trying to minimize. An equally poor choice for an aging neck is the high round or jewel neckline, since it acts as a frame for the problem area (figure 9).

There are ways to flatter a neck that is no longer young. One way is to wear an open-necked collar with a high stand. For a softer, less tailored look, try easy, wide turtlenecks, cowl necks or blouses edged in soft ruffles or ruching (figures 10, 11 and 12).

Too Short

Many women with short necks are convinced that the best way to deal with the problem is to cover them up. In reality, the very opposite is true. The more you bare a short neck, the better it will look. The best thing you can do is dress your short neck with V shapes, open necklines and collars that lie flat (figures 13, 14 and 15).

Short necks look unattractive in styles that have horizontal detail-

Do !

Figs. 13, 14, 15

Don't!

ing across the shoulders, in turtlenecks or in garments with stand-up sleeves (figures 16, 17 and 18). These will make the neck appear shorter than it really is. Another no-no is long hair, which shortens the appearance of the neck by resting on the shoulders. Hair that is worn up or cut short will create the illusion of added length to the neck and will look more attractive. The opposite is true when wearing jewelry. Necklaces should hang low on the neck rather than tight around the neck.

SHOULDERS

Width in the shoulders can be a great asset, but the overly broad kind may present a problem. The best solution, if this is your problem, is to emphasize vertical lines. A halter look is a good example. Nothing is lovelier by night than a broad, bare back of a woman. The right halter can be one of the nicest things a woman can do for her broad-shouldered torso (figure 19).

Another way to break up the wide expanse from shoulder to

Do !

Figs. 19, 20, 21

Don't

Figs. 22, 23, 24

shoulder is with vests, tunics, jumpers or tailored jackets that have set-in shoulder seams (figures 20 and 21). Styles with horizontal lines, like off-the-shoulder tops, boat necks or puffed sleeves with fussy, horizontal detail, don't look good on this type of figure (figures 22, 23 and 24). Any garment that has a narrow shoulder helps to camouflage a broad shoulder problem. Another tip for you is to make sure shoulder seams never extend beyond the shoulder bone.

A problem shared by many women are shoulders that are intrinsically narrow or that slope due to poor posture. In an effort to de-emphasize their height when they were young, tall girls often have developed poor posture. They let their shoulders droop instead of standing up straight.

If your shoulders are narrow and/or have the tendency to slope,

Do !

Figs. 25, 26, 27

Figs. 28, 29, 30

look for shapes that rise slightly above them. Puffed sleeves and jackets with shoulder pads work well. If your jackets don't have the built-in variety, they can be purchased in most notions departments (figures 25, 26 and 27).

Avoid dresses with droopy, off-the-shoulder sleeves and styles that combine tight tops with big skirts; they will make you look like a pear. Blouses with drop shoulders and dolman sleeves only serve to emphasize your dilemma (figures 28, 29 and 30).

ARMS

A good-looking, well-toned arm is a great asset. Unfortunately, there aren't many of them around. Arms fall victim to all kinds of problems quite early in life. They can be overly muscular from too

$Do\,!$

much exercise, too scrawny from the lack of exercise and advancing age will make them appear flabby. You already know what makes them fat.

Many performers, aware of these problems, prefer to keep their arms under wraps on the theory that anything less than the best should remain hidden.

The most effective camouflage for a heavy arm is easy-fitting sleeves. Full sleeves and off-the-shoulder shapes work well, and, since heavy arms often come with a well-padded chest, you might dress to make the most of both those attributes. Wear wide open necklines (figures 31, 32 and 33). There are a couple of Hungarian sisters in Hollywood who have been doing that successfully for years. They've had everyone so intrigued by what's on top, few know or care what goes on below the bust.

Tight sleeves will look and feel uncomfortable (figure 34). Elastic and other types of bindings will cut into the flesh, and, since short sleeves invariably emphasize the heaviest part of the arm, it is best to avoid them altogether (figure 35).

Heavy arms left totally bare are not particularly attractive, especially since they are also (usually) accompanied by heavy folds of flesh around the armpits (figure 36).

The best way to turn skinny arms from a liability into an asset is to put them in proportion with the rest of your body by wearing fuller sleeves. Thin arms look best when covered with blouses, dresses or sweaters that have long, full sleeves, especially those that are tight at the wrist (figures 37, 38 and 39). Wide, short sleeves, as well as bare

Don't!

Figs. 34, 35, 36

Do !

Figs. 37, 38, 39

Don't !

Figs. 40, 41, 42

and sleeveless tops, will make arms appear even skinnier. The same applies to skimpy sweaters, which will draw attention to the very area that ought to be hidden (figures 40, 41 and 42).

BUST

The saying that marriage is like a bird cage because those who are in, want out, and those who are out, want in, applies to a lot more than the state of matrimony. Women with straight hair go to great lengths to acquire curls, and many shorties would prefer to be tall; every paleface dreams of a golden tan.

Many women feel the same way about their bust. Those who are small feel cheated, while others, who are overendowed, would give anything to fit into a 34B. To be perfectly candid those women with smaller busts wear clothes better. First of all, there are fewer fitting problems. Besides, a little here and there can always be added, but taking away is quite another matter.

Being generously endowed can have its compensations. You might well have an upper torso worth baring. Just look at what that

Raquel Welch.

Harry Langdon Photography

Figs. 43, 44, 45

Do !

has done for Liz Taylor, Raquel Welch and some of the other stars. While I realize that you cannot walk around at all hours of the day revealing your cleavage, there are other steps you can take to minimize an overly generous bustline. Loosely fitting jackets or cardigans are a good solution, as are softly ruffled, off-the-shoulder tops. Blouses or shirts with V-necks also work well (figures 43, 44 and 45). On the other hand, overemphasizing an ample bust will make you appear too obvious. Long chains that disappear into your cleavage, stiff fabrics that stand out from the body or form-fitting dresses will certainly make you stand out, but not stylishly. T-shirts also call attention to the well-endowed woman, perhaps too much attention (figures 46, 47 and 48).

Most important of all is to find the right bra, the kind that is smooth and will give you sufficient support without cutting into the flesh. Some underwire bras are excellent, especially the kind with side-control panels. There are also any number of long-line styles that can give excellent support and that are preferred by some women over the shorter variety.

The torpedo-shaped, up-and-out, cantilevered bra is not recommended because all it achieves is a rather exaggerated, unnatural appearance.

Figs. 46, 47, 48

WAIST

According to Webster's, the waist is that part of the human body that lies between the ribs and the hips, "usually the narrowest part of the torso." That is, I suppose, as apt a description as any, except that it fails to mention the fact that not all waists are necessarily narrow.

As a matter of fact, most waists fall into three distinct categories —long, short and in-between. The latter presents few problems, so I will confine my recommendations to the first two.

At the outset, it is important to establish the fact that short waists are not the exclusive province of short figures. They can happen to tall women as well. Yet all short-waisted bodies have one thing in common—they're difficult to fit. They look best in "no-waist" dresses,

Do !

Figs. 49, 50, 51

like empires, or in unfitted jackets, vests or blazers (figures 49, 50 and 51). Anyone whose waist is on the short side ought to shun tops with horizontal detailing, dresses that call attention to the waist, most belts—especially the wide ones—tight T-shirts and, above all, bare midriffs. This is because many short-waisted women are victims of the midriff bulge (figures 52, 53 and 54). If you must wear a two-piece outfit, make sure the color of the top and bottom match to avoid that "cut through the middle" look.

Like her short-waisted sister, the long-waisted woman looks great in unfitted or empire-style dresses. She will look spectacular in high-waisted pants and wide belts. On her, sashes can be very attractive.

Don't!

Do !

If you are long waisted and also have short legs, your plight is shared by many. It is a common occurrence. To compensate for this problem it is important to reinforce an illusion of length in the legs by raising the waistline, or, if need be, by eliminating it altogether (figures 55, 56 and 57). Tops with a strong vertical design are a poor choice.

Figs. 55, 56, 57

This is also true of any style that has a low-waist detail. Overblouses and garments that end below the waist and blousons (figures 58, 59 and 60) are examples of this.

To give your legs the longest possible look skirts should be worn below the knee with shoes that have heels.

Figs. 58, 59, 60

Figs. 61, 62, 63

Do !

HIPS

Imagine having to complain about hips that are simply not wide enough. How many women would love to have that problem? Yet there are figures with hips so narrow that they appear to have no waist at all, and, to compound the problem, thighs that look as though they are bulging at the sides. If this happens to be your plight, flatter your shape with overblouses that are belted at the waist to achieve a peplumlike fullness at the hips, with peg-topped skirts or with straight-

Figs. 64, 65, 66

cut pants that have pleats and side pockets. These are designed to improve your proportions by adding a little extra fullness to the hipline (figures 61, 62 and 63).

Stay away from tightly fitted pants and other form-fitting garments that will only serve to accentuate your shortcoming. While blouson tops worn with straight pants or skirts can be flattering, make sure they don't look top-heavy, especially if your hips are exceptionally slim (figures 64, 65 and 66).

Don't!

Do !

As many of you know only too well, being somewhat broad in the beam is a fate shared by thousands of women the world over, and, while this may not be much of a consolation, knowing how to cope with the problem can make all the difference. To de-emphasize very full, round hips (which are, as often as not, attached to a full, round derriere) your best bet is to wear high-waisted, flowing

Figs. 67, 68, 69

Figs. 70, 71, 72

garments. Full or A-line skirts and pants that are cut straight from the hip (figures 67, 68 and 69) will flatter your shape.

Bear in mind that any fullness should always start at the widest part of the hip. Never accentuate those generous proportions by decking them out in tightly fitting, waist-cinching skirts or dresses, or worse, by stuffing them into snuggly-fitting bell-bottoms (figures 70, 71 and 72). Avoid figure-hugging bodices of any kind.

Don't!

LEGS

American women are widely praised for the beauty of their long, shapely legs. Unfortunately, not every American woman is so blessed. If your gams leave something to be desired, don't despair. There are several ways to improve their appearance. By and large, legs—like hips—tend to fall into two basic categories—the heavy and the skinny.

Some of the world's most ravishing-looking bodies are attached to a sturdy set of legs. If you happen to fall into this particular category, the best thing you can do is draw attention away from them and make them appear slimmer by matching the color of your hose to that of your shoes, or, better yet, match both shoes and hose to the color of your skirt. This is particularly effective whenever you are wearing colors that are on the dark side.

Do !

Figs. 73, 74, 75, 76

In the summertime your best colors will be beige or neutral shades. Another way to enhance the appearance of your stocky legs is by wearing the right shoes. Flat, close-toed pumps or simple espadrilles with a wedge are excellent when worn with pants and other leisure clothes. Sandals or plain pumps with a two- or three-inch heel look smart with skirts and dresses (figures 73–76).

Beware of spike heels! They will only serve to emphasize the heaviness of the leg. Stay away from extremely light or extremely dark hose. Hose with patterns attract the eye and call attention to your legs, and flashy, gimmicky shoes, clunky oxfords or platforms with extra thick, colorful soles are not flattering to heavy legs (figures 77 and 78).

Dainty shoes and sandals, (figures 79 and 80) which look so sexy in store windows, are not for you. They can spell instant disaster

Don't!

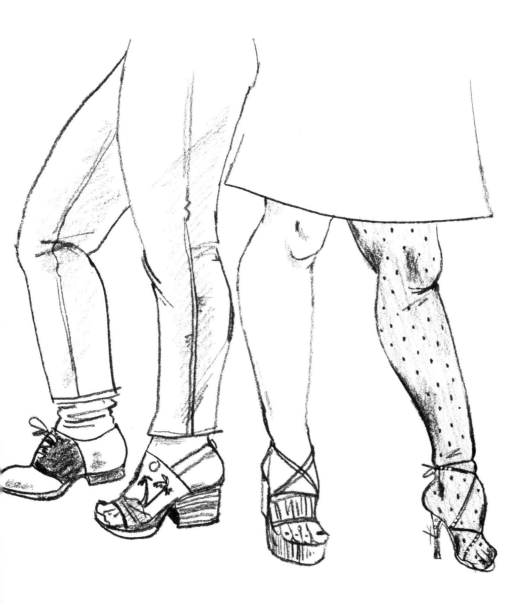

Figs. 77, 78, 79, 80

on any but the shapeliest of feet and ankles. What could be more ludicrous than an amply endowed lady, blessed with a pair of sturdy legs, tottering down the street in strippy sandals with five-inch heels, looking to all the world as though she is trying to defy gravity.

One more point: Since heavy legs often go with chubby knees, it makes good sense to avoid wearing anything above the knee. You should also select only those pants that are straight cut.

Skinny legs are the perfect foil for dainty, simple pumps or sandals. Both of these will look better with higher heels, because they make the foot look smaller (figures 81 and 82).

For active sports a small-scale, lightweight shoe, worn with a lightweight sock, or a pair of low-heeled, barefoot sandals are your most flattering footwear (figures 83 and 84). Skinny legs that run into bulky, busy, flat clunkers are very unattractive (figures 85–88). Another factor that will strongly affect the overall appearance of your legs is skirt length. A hem that is too long will make skinny legs look like match sticks, and a skirt that is too short may well reveal a set of knobby knees.

Do !

Figs. 81, 82, 83, 84

Figs. 85, 86, 87, 88

THE LENGTH OF THE HEM

Nothing affects the appearance of the figure more drastically than a hemline, and no single fashion topic has caused more controversy over the years. If we are to believe the predictions of a few designers, we might even see the return of the mini.

At the risk of incurring the wrath of fashion mavens everywhere, I'll stick my neck out and state that the best hemline for most women is the just-below-the-knees version. Regardless of past, current or future trends, this length is by far the most flattering. A hem that ends up six or seven inches below the knee may look great draped on a tall, lanky body blessed with long shapely legs, but it's a disaster for the less than slender leg because it hits at its most vulnerable part, making it appear even heavier. I have already mentioned what it does to skinny legs and that it makes short women look as though they're wearing their big sisters' clothes.

I've tried it on Carol Burnett, a lady with a pair of extremely shapely legs and dainty ankles, but it didn't work. All I had to do to make her look gawky was to dress her in something that hit her at mid-calf, add a pair of funny-looking shoes, and presto! Instant disaster. Good for some hearty laughs from the audience, yet anything but flattering from a fashion point of view.

TALL WOMEN

There is something absolutely wonderful about tall women. They look stunning in their clothes, providing they take advantage of their figure by practicing good posture and by being proud of their height. If you're tall, don't try to hide it. Instead, wear the kind of clothes that tend to emphasize and dramatize your body. Large, bulky jackets; long, free-flowing scarves; huge, flaring sleeves; the layered look; capes; ponchos; all these dramatic styles will glorify your height (figures 89, 90 and 91).

Figs. 89, 90, 91

Always make sure that details, including collars, buttons and ties are proportioned to your size. Wear high heels, even if you're dating a shorter man. After all, he knew you were tall when he asked you out. The only thing you will accomplish by wearing flat shoes is to make your feet look bigger.

Three-quarter sleeves, short skirts or skimpy, tight-fitting tops and pants (figures 92 and 93) are no good for you. With these clothes you will simply emphasize your height in the wrong way. Don't attempt to look five feet two inches, unless you don't mind looking like

Don't !

Figs. 92, 93, 94

an overgrown Shirley Temple. Avoid dainty, overly fussy clothes or clothes that look as if they're too short (figure 94).

SHORT WOMEN

A perfectly proportioned "shortie" will be able to wear just about anything as long as it is scaled down to her height. The best styles to look for are those that give the longest, possible vertical line—non-waisted dresses, princess styles or tailored coordinates with a minimum of construction.

The most flattering necklines are those that are low and open (figures 95, 96 and 97). The colors of your skirts, blouses and sweaters should match to avoid that "cut-off" look. If you must wear a belt, find a soft self-sash and try tying it just below instead of right at the waist.

Do !

Figs. 95, 96, 97

Figs. 98, 99, 100

Beware of ruffles, puffed sleeves and lots of bouncy curls in your hair. I have known quite a few very pretty girls who are short, but due to their lack of height, they have developed a severe case of the cutes. This happens well beyond the age when that sort of look is acceptable. They invariably ended up looking like so many potential "Baby Janes." If you are petite, avoid large patterns, such as plaids or oversized flowery prints. Remember that contrasting colors that are worn in horizontal combinations will emphasize your lack of height. Heavily tailored coats and jackets with oversized collars, bulky turtlenecks and other heavy garments will totally overwhelm your figure (figures 98, 99 and 100).

Stay away from long hemlines and oversized accessories—including hats, jewelry or handbags—and, when it comes to your hairstyle, wear it short or up. Don't let it rest on your shoulders.

Don't!

ON BEING OVERWEIGHT

Now we come to a problem that is an obsession of national proportions. Men and women weigh more today than they have for a decade, according to numerous magazine and newspaper articles. There are all sorts of dreary statistics about our collective flab. According to the experts, we eat too much, and, as if that weren't enough in itself, we eat too much of the wrong food—food that is rich and fattening. In addition, we don't get enough exercise. After all this, we have a compulsive need to take up one fad diet after another.

I'm all for slim. It's healthy, it looks attractive and it's sexy. But let's face it, lot's of people aren't slim. The abundance and the quality of the food they eat, combined with a relaxed life-style, has overwhelmed them; yet, they still manage to look great. How do they do it?

Of all figure problems none is more serious or more difficult to compensate for than too much weight. I'm not talking about the size 8 who has blossomed into a size 12. True overweight begins where the daily struggle with the bathroom scale leaves off and the search for good-looking clothes has become a hassle.

If this is your problem, never lose sight of the fact that size is more than a number. Nothing is more fattening or less flattering than a too-tight fit. It will add an instant ten pounds to what is already there. Be realistic. Don't try to squeeze into the size you would like to be. Twelve may sound better than sixteen, but if sixteen is where you're at, don't settle for less. You will end up looking better, trimmer and feeling more comfortable in your actual size.

Making the Least of the Most

Clothes are wonderful. They can pick you up when you're down. They can make you feel sexy, desirable, demure and beautiful. They can do anything you want them to do, whether you're a trim six or a regal sixteen. The key is in learning how to make them work for you, so let's look at the options for the woman who is overweight.

If you prefer to keep your shape under wraps and are tall enough to carry it off, caftans and generously proportioned tunics can be marvelously versatile. They are available in a variety of styles and fabrics and are designed to look as good on the beach as they do in the ballroom or in the boudoir. However, unless you're five feet eight or over, these are not for you.

Caftans can make the short, heavy woman look like a mountain of fabric (figure 105). You are better off with other loosely shaped garments, such as a smock or tent dress (figure 102), empire styles (especially good if you happen to have a pretty bust), skirts that flare and wrap or amply proportioned pants that are worn with an overblouse or a loosely fitted jacket long enough to cover both hips and derriere (figures 101 and 103).

Whatever you do, avoid anything that is fitted, frilly, fussy or stretchy, and don't wear tight pants! Shorts, sleeveless tops, bare midriffs and dainty jewelry (figures 104 and 106) are also taboo.

Not only does the shape of your garment make a difference in the way you look, but so does the fabric of which it is made. Your

Do !

Figs. 101, 102, 103

Figs. 104, 105, 106

clothes should be soft, but should not cling to your body. Sheer wools, challises, double knits, some silks, chiffons and crepes are good materials to use. Avoid heavy tweeds, bulky knits, big furs or rigid fabrics such as linen, taffetas or brocades. These will only add to what is already there.

While trying to make more look like less, don't overlook the importance of colors and patterns. There is no question that muted shades are more slimming than bright ones and that subdued prints are more flattering than big, splashy ones. Vertical pinstripes are excellent (avoid horizontal stripes, of course), and, if you must wear checks or plaids, make them small and understated.

The use of monochromatic colors (for hose and shoes too) will create an illusion of slimness. Contrasting shades will make you appear shorter and heavier.

The overweight woman should also avoid hair that is too long.

There is no doubt that being overweight is a burden, but if you have lost the battle of the bulge and you have resigned yourself to the status quo, try making the problem work for you by selecting clothes that are designed to draw attention away from your figure.

IT'S IN THE BAG

No chapter on clothes would be complete without a few words about handbags, a topic likely to arouse even more passionate responses than the section on skirt length. Tell a woman her skirt is too long and she may do one of two things—shorten it or ignore your advice. If she ignores it, she will probably do so on the theory that you haven't kept up with your fashion reading and, therefore, don't really know what you're talking about. But confront her with the fact that her bag is too large and you're asking for trouble. You are attacking a highly prized, personal object.

I've never been able to figure out that strange attachment women form to those oversized appendages, which weigh enough to dislocate an elbow. If you happen to be a professional model or have the build of an Amazon, bigger may be better. Otherwise, a handbag—like everything else in your wardrobe—should be in proportion to the rest of you, and, with all due respect to Messrs. Gucci and Vuitton, I also happen to believe that bags should be functional first and fashionable second. They ought to be roomy enough to hold what you need without being cluttered or oversized. A good-quality leather bag is an indispensable item in any wardrobe. It is one of the best investments you can make. If one is all you can afford, select one in a neutral shade that will go with everything you own.

SUMMING UP

There is really only one way to find out what looks good on you and that is to try it on. Different clothes work for different people and there are no hard-and-fast rules to follow, except these:

1. Never buy anything simply because it looks good on someone else.

2. Don't be fooled by those mannequins in store windows. Those dummies are a perfectly proportioned size ten and would look good in a used flour sack.

3. Never buy something just because it's on sale. The season's most persuasive mark-down will turn out to be a loser whenever you substitute price for the right look or the proper fit.

CHAPTER FIVE

The Magic of Color

Redheads

As a designer, I use color to establish a mood, create a dramatic look or convey an emotion. Color has a strong impact on performers and audiences alike, and, because of this, I have to be very careful in the selection. The wrong hue on a performer can ruin a scene or spoil a musical number. A bubbly singer with a repertoire of upbeat songs would look as ludicrous in somber black as would the heroine in a Shakespearean tragedy all done up in shocking pink or orange. Colors must be picked objectively; they must not be allowed to overshadow the personality or natural coloring of the wearer.

It is surprising how many people avoid wearing certain colors because they have been told they look bad in them. This may not be true at all. The way to find out which shades will work for you is to test them against your hair and skin in natural daylight. The fluorescent lighting found in stores tends to distort the colors.

Women rarely feel good wearing a color they dislike, even though that particular shade might actually look very good on them. It is easy to lose sight of the fact that you wear colors as much for others to enjoy as you do for yourself. You should learn to enjoy the colors that enhance your looks, even if they are not your favorites.

On the other hand, your favorite colors might not look good on you. That's not to say you can't still wear them, but try to use them to accessorize your clothes. While a scarf, belt or a piece of jewelry won't dominate your appearance, it may add just the right touch to whatever you happen to be wearing.

Surrounding yourself with the colors you enjoy is important. If you happen to love reds, oranges and yellows, but don't wear them well, why not use them in your home? You will be creating a setting in which you will be seen, and the colors you enjoy will flatter your personality, which is important in decorating your home or office.

Certain shades are more difficult to wear than others. This is especially true of the stronger colors, such as magenta, purple, royal blue, lime green and—in some cases—black. White, on the opposite side, is flattering to almost anyone, except those who have a very pale skin. Off-white, beige or bone is softer and even more flattering than pure white. One thing to bear in mind when wearing white is that it demands attention. If you are the only woman at a party dressed all in white, you are bound to be noticed.

Climate affects the choice of colors we wear. In colder environments warm yellows, vibrant reds and shocking pinks are out of place, but they are perfect for warm, sunny places where everything, including the flowers and sky, is brighter. Many people who live in sunny climes have dark skins and look great in exotic hues that complement them and their surroundings. Stunning African colors lose their beauty under grey, cloudy skies, just as a southern California wardrobe may be out of place in the wintry streets of New York or Boston. Nature provides a background for the colors we choose, and we should choose the proper colors for the setting.

People are becoming increasingly aware and sophisticated about the use of color. They are willing to experiment. This is especially true of the ethnic groups, who look better for having returned to the colors of their origins. These clothes are more compatible with their personalities and their complexions.

To make it easy for you to find out what your own best colors are I have devoted each section in this chapter to a specific type, ranging from the fairest blonde to the richest black.

BLONDES

The world is full of blondes. Some are natural, others are not. To me most blondes look good in blue—from the palest to the deepest navy—with an occasional touch of red. Sometimes a very fair blonde looks great in a bright, clear red or a blonde beige. It gives them that "blonde all over" look. The type of blonde who has the tendency to appear washed out can perk up her appearance with some carefully applied make-up.

There are basically two types of natural blondes—those who have fair hair, blue eyes and a very light complexion, such as Cheryl Ladd, and blondes such as Goldie Hawn, who have golden skin to go with their golden hair.

I prefer dressing Goldie in off-white, golden beige and yellow for an "all in one" look. This type of blonde looks wonderful in all the warm shades—rusts, corals, pinks and browns. Because Goldie tans better than a paler blonde does, she looks sensational in white. She

Goldie Hawn.

should, however, stay away from purples to avoid a jaundiced look.

I believe most blondes look good in soft pastels and, of course, in black. A very fair blonde should be careful not to be overwhelmed by very bright, harsh shades of orange, purple, royal blue and lime green. A blonde is wiser to stick to a more subtle palette.

Gold jewelry is my choice for blondes, though silver can look sensational on a tan, flaxen beauty. I love to see blondes in turquoise or lapis lazuli. Then, of course, there's Carol Channing, who has always recommended diamonds.

BRUNETTES

Brown-haired women are the majority in this country. Some are fair complexioned with dark brown hair like Marie Osmond, and others have medium brown hair and medium complexions like Barbra Streisand. There are also pale-complexioned girls with light brown hair (Phyllis George) and the olive-skinned beauties with either brown or very dark hair (Raquel Welch and Cher).

Not all women are pleased with their brown hair. They alter the color, sometimes rather drastically. Some browns are somewhat drab, but it is usually more flattering to change the original shade gently, perhaps to a richer chestnut, or to add subtle light streaks. A reddish brown can do a lot to pep up your appearance, and a dull medium brown can be changed into a ravishing dark chocolate.

Women with medium brown hair and medium complexions can wear almost every color. I like them in warm rusts, browns, beiges and warm reds. One of Barbra Streisand's favorite colors is mauve. She makes it work for her by adding touches of it to her face and eye make-up. This is a rather sophisticated method of making a color work for you, but one that is available to everyone. Thanks to the tremendous variety of colors on sale in every drug and department store, women can use make-up to enhance and reinforce almost any color they enjoy wearing, as long as it's applied carefully and sparingly.

Women with medium brown hair usually wear black or white well and look sensational dressed in beige. Brown hair looks great with gold jewelry, coral, jade, tiger's eye, carnelian, topaz and tortoiseshell.

The fair-skinned, dark- or black-haired girl will appear vibrant in rich, bright colors, such as purple, magenta, orange, coral, emerald, teal and my favorite for her—red. She will also find clear pastels are flattering to her complexion and she can look simply stunning in black or white. Very drab colors are not the best choice. She will look good in most types of jewelry—there's nothing like white gold, diamonds or rubies to really cheer her up.

If you're the Raquel type with brown hair and olive skin, you'll look great in beige, off-white, brown and different shades of orange, such as shrimp, coral and vermilion. Certain light teal blues can also be exciting. In the summer your hair and skin may almost match and the tawny approach to dressing can be dramatic.

Very dark-haired, olive-skinned ladies will look sensational in black or white. By and large, olive complexions can carry off extremes far better than most and they look great in bright, exotic shades or interesting muted pastels. I don't really like them in some of the more neutral shades, like olive, certain beiges and some camels, because they tend to bring out the yellow in the skin. Shades of purple should also be chosen carefully.

Olive-skinned girls look good in gold or silver jewelry. In fact, I like a combination of the two. Coral, tiger's eye, turquoise, ivory and carnelian are also flattering.

John Engstead

(Left) Cher. (Right) Phyllis George.

Harry Langdon Photography

REDHEADS

Red hair is very exciting. If you are a mousy-haired girl with pale skin and a few freckles, red hair can give you a new lease on life. Redheads can use their hair as a built-in color guide. All you have to do is look at colors that are an extension of your own hair—rust, salmon or brown.

Contrary to common belief, redheads can look sensational in certain shades of red, but they are often timid about experimenting because they have always been told that red is a color they should not wear. I love them in red burgundy, but they look equally super in orange-red. Most shades of green and blue are flattering to titian

Exotics

tresses, and, while plum or purple may sound garish, I've seen these colors looking great on women with red hair.

As you know, there is nothing as stunning as a fair-skinned, natural redhead dressed in emerald green, a color many redheads would just as soon avoid. It's understandable, because that's what their mothers loved to dress them in when they were little girls. But, if they can overcome the deja vu, it is one of a redhead's best color combinations.

And then, of course, there's black. It can be very dramatic against a background of milky white skin with bright rust hair.

While redheads and emeralds are made for each other, topaz, tiger's eye, coral, carnelian or jade can be just as effective.

BLACK WOMEN

Black women at large have many different skin tones, ranging from a lovely olive to a soft, rich ebony. Those women with a lot of yellow in their skin tone should avoid golds, olive greens and purples. Dark skins look lovely in rich, vibrant shades, in muted pastels and in soft beiges and browns.

While I do like black women in black or white, I prefer not to dress them in navy or dark grey. The beautiful color combinations worn by black women in Africa could well serve as an example to their westernized sisters, as well as to members of other ethnic groups. Black, Latin and Oriental women could well look to their origins for their best and most flattering colors. They should take advantage of the beautiful authentic fabrics and jewelry that have been developed and perfected over centuries.

SILVER-HAIRED WOMEN

Grey hair is softening to the effects of advancing age. It can be both beautiful and flattering. But not all women want to be grey, and not all grey is attractive. I'm all in favor of covering it up, providing the new shade is soft and slightly lighter than what was the original pregrey hue.

Another good way to liven up drab-looking grey hair (or yellowed white hair) is to use a rinse or to add lighter streaks.

If your hair is grey, you may not be able to wear some colors as well as you did with your original shade. If you used to look great in browns, you may now find that shades of grey tend to be more flattering.

I like women with grey hair dressed in rich, clear colors, as well as in grey, white, or black. However, if you do wear black, be sure to soften its effect by adding touches of white or some other light color around your face. Most pastels are okay. Just make sure you're not walking around looking like those sweet blue-haired ladies in their Easter-egg colored dresses.

Purple on women with grey or white hair is nice. While I am aware that people tend to think of purple and lavender as old lady colors, they can really look very beautiful, as long as the woman can feel good wearing them and can rid herself of the Victorian taboo against purple and lavender.

All colors of jewelry are good with grey hair, but perhaps silver is the most flattering of all.

SUMMING UP

There is more to color than meets the eye. It tells others something about the way you feel, the mood you are in and the image you are trying to project. As long as the shades you select flatter your hair and complexion, colors can go a long way to enhance your appearance.

Don't wear a color simply because it happens to be this season's "thing." Each season brings another color to the forefront of fashion, but, unless it happens to look good on you, you're better off ignoring the fad.

Silver Grey

PART THREE

Stars That Shine

My contacts with the following stars are purely professional, although I am friends with all of them. However, I am not going to give you gossip or fascinating, lurid stories about their private lives and loves; it is primarily the working relationship I am going to talk to you about. I think you will find these visual vignettes interesting, and I know you will like each of them as much as I do.

What I think I like best about working with these glamourous women is the constant change and development taking place in them —and in me—over the years. Each performer brings with her a definite personality, and as she changes and grows I, too, have an opportunity to grow.

Ann-Margret in "The Villain"

CHAPTER SIX

Introducing the Ladies

A design for Lee Remick as the Stripping Mermaid.

My career working with the stars began in the mid-sixties when Ray Aghayan and I were designing for the stars who appeared on a series of television specials called "Danny Thomas's Wonderful World of Burlesque." With each new show a group of performers arrived whom we were to transform into baggy-pants comics, exotic strippers, cute soubrettes and sophisticated ladies. The time period for each new show was set anywhere between the turn-of-the-century and the 1940's war years. This wide range of eras gave us a lot of exciting possibilities to work with.

On the first show we changed "all-American girl" **Lee Remick** into a singing, dancing soubrette of the 1920s, then into a sultry, stripping mermaid and, finally, into a lovely lady who rode a crescent moon over the audience and snapped her garters at the bald heads in the front row.

It was also on these shows that I first designed costumes for such performers as Carol Channing, Nanette Fabray, Cyd Charisse, Juliet Prowse, Shirley Jones and dozens of chorus cuties. And, oh, I must not forget the most perfect "talking woman" and burlesque queen of them all, **Lucille Ball**.

All my life I have been a fan of Lucy's. At our first meeting I was terrified into silence; Ray wound up doing all the talking, while I made suggestions from the background. Lucy is a formidable lady who commands and deserves great respect, and to this day I tend to be a little shy around her.

On one of these specials, Lucy was asked to portray a turn-of-the-century lady performing as a monarch butterfly. The director decided

Lee Remick as the Lady in the Moon.

that Lucy should *fly* over the audience on a wire, doing somersaults at the same time. The producers brought in Peter Foy, the flying genius who originally rigged Mary Martin to make her fly in "Peter Pan." Lucy had only one week to become a dazzling butterfly, and the harness she had to wear was not only bulky and uncomfortable, it was also very painful. But Lucy worked hard to get it right. Dressed in a wasp-waist leotard of the period, with high-laced green-and-yellow silk boots and giant, china-silk butterfly wings (which I personally painted with transparent dyes), Lucy was a vision. She fluttered over the crowd as if she had been born to fly.

Probably the first performer I felt truly comfortable with was **Nanette Fabray**. Nanette is one of the dearest and funniest women in the business. I first met her on the "Danny Thomas Show," and I have been fortunate enough to work with her several times since, not only on a number of Carol Burnett shows, but also on a ninety-minute special entitled "Alice Through the Looking Glass."

Nanette is a costume designer's dream because she allows them to make her look good or bad, as long as it's right for the part. On "Alice Through the Looking Glass" Nanette played the Wacky White Queen. The late Agnes Moorehead was the Red Queen, with Ricardo Montalban and the British actor, Robert Coote, portraying the White and Red Kings.

The costumes for the red and white monarchy were very heavy and extremely uncomfortable, and with all the constant technical stops needed in shooting a show of this kind, the actors were forced to wear these cumbersome outfits for hours on end. We did everything we could to try to ease their misery, everything but remove the entire costumes, which would have taken a great deal of time, and on any set 'time is money.' The two actors spent the entire time groaning and bemoaning their predicament, while the two ladies bore the pain stoically, waiting for the next shot. You'll never make me believe that women are the weaker sex!

In 1966 I was hired to design my first nightclub act only because the star couldn't have the designer she wanted. The star was **Mitzi Gaynor**, and we have worked together ever since. Mitzi and I have had a good time over the years: I understand her, how she moves and how she works. She trusts me to know what is best for her.

Mitzi was really the first performer to take a chance on me for something as important as her nightclub clothes. These kinds of costumes are worn for at least one year or more and they have to be perfect in every way. When we first met, the fashion silhouette of the day was changing from long to mini skirts, from fitted waists to easy, unfitted shapes. High spiked heels were being replaced by either very low pumps or vinyl boots. The 'mod' look of the mid-sixties may have been perfect on Twiggy, but it was a bit of a problem for Mitzi, whose measurements are 36-22-36. So I designed a mini-dress for her that had princess seaming, which eased in and out with the curves of her body, as opposed to the straight cardboard-box look of the time. Her sensational legs were a great plus. At our first meeting I got carried away, showing her six different sketches for each change of costume and, much to my dismay, she decided to have them all made up. She had a choice of six spangled mini-dresses in red, pink, yellow, orange, black or white. To this day these still remain her favorite colors, with bright pink in the number-one spot.

I soon realized that Mitzi loved clothes and liked to have lots of them. All of her gowns must have the same kind of outgoing exuberance she radiates. Mitzi has a terrific sense of humor and a superb feeling for the theatrical. She enjoys handling the most complicated and outrageous clothes. I can dress her in a skirt with one hundred yards in

(Opposite) Nanette Fabray and friend. (Above) Mitzi Gaynor and her minis.

the hem and she will move as if it were a few ounces of tulle. She not only has great individual style and a marvelous figure, but she is one of the the funniest women I know. Working with Mitzi is always a joy.

My first encounter with **Linda Hopkins** took place in 1976 while designing Mitzi Gaynor's TV special, "Mitzi! Roarin' in the Twenties." Linda Hopkins was a guest on the special, and I was to make her look like a Bessie Smith-type speakeasy singer of the 1920s.

Well, it doesn't take too much to make Linda look like a Bessie Smith type. I came up with a purple panne velvet evening gown of the period, with a heavily jeweled bodice and a silk fringe skirt. During the fitting, Linda squealed with delight like a little girl in her first Sunday dress, but on stage she was anything but a little girl. She strutted, she

(Above) A design for Linda Hopkins. (Right) Linda Hopkins. (Opposite) Mitzi Gaynor.

Photo by David Vance

shimmied, she shook and did she sing! I love doing clothes for Linda, because nobody enjoys dressing up as much as she does.

An exquisite dancing star who started her career in film musicals is **Cyd Charisse**. I recall sitting at the movies for hours on end, watching her dance her way through dozens of MGM musicals. So, when the time came for us to meet, I was a bit intimidated, but her friendly and gracious manner soon put me at ease.

I quickly learned that making Cyd Charisse look good was easy. She has one of the all-time great bodies, and, of course, her legs are phenomenal. A designer should consider himself lucky to have Cyd wearing his clothes. I've dressed many dancers over the years and believe I have a feeling for their particular art.

Probably the most exciting dancer today in musical theater and nightclubs is **Juliet Prowse**. She is one of those amazing performers who looks best when she is wearing very little. Because her body is so well-toned and has such a beautiful shape she can wear almost nothing and never look offensive.

Juliet started dancing professionally when she was a teenager, and, to this day, she has managed to maintain a high degree of discipline as a dancer and performer. Besides being a fabulous dancer, she's a born quick-change artist, who can make an off-stage costume change from the skin out, including a wig change, in mere seconds. Some of her changes are so incredibly fast you'd swear she was twins!

Juliet Prowse.
(Opposite) Cyd Charisse.

Speaking of nudity and Juliet, on a TV special a few years ago, she was required to dance a number portraying three jewels: diamond, sapphire and ruby. For it, I devised a nude-colored bodysuit of mesh, completely covered in rhinestones of different sizes. Over this basic costume she had to wear bits and pieces signifying the jewel she was portraying at that moment—a very heavy plot at best.

She did her turn as the diamond, with the swirling strips of diamonds engulfing her fabulous body, followed by a very ethereal sapphire in yards of chiffon in many shades of blue. Then came the ruby, the most seductive segment of all. The taping was going along smoothly—no split seams and everything looked beautiful—when, suddenly, I was called to the technical booth by a very worried looking secretary. Juliet's ruby costume, which completely covered her nude bodystocking, appeared on the camera as though the poor girl was up there dancing without her drawers. The censor lady was about to faint, the producer was having a fit, I thought it looked kind of neat and Juliet kept on dancing. Something, needless to say, had to be done. While no extra fabric to match the ruby color was available, I did discover a red metallic candy wrapper on the floor. I rushed to the candy machine to buy as many Rocky Road candy bars as I had quarters for. Then, with

Harry Langdon Photography

Juliet Prowse

(Above) A design for Juliet Prowse. (Opposite) Juliet Prowse.

tiny safety pins, we attached red candy wrappers in all the appropriate places. The censor lady revived, the producer calmed down and Juliet just kept on dancing.

Often a one-shot deal becomes a long-term involvement, and that's what happened with the Supremes. I was hired to do the clothes for a special television show called "**Diana Ross** and the Supremes and the Temptations on Broadway." Whew! The Supremes' regular designer was unavailable, so I was brought in to create the costumes for this spectacular event. I can truthfully say it was one of the most enjoyable projects I've ever worked on.

Since they were known for their glitter and flash, I had a free hand in designing some really smashing clothes. The results were an Emmy for me and the pleasure of inheriting Diana as a client after she left the Supremes to go on her own. We have worked together almost continuously since then, and each season she returns from her tour with wonderful ideas about the ways she wants to look.

I'm sure that as a child Diana must have spent hours in front of a mirror practicing how to be a star. I can dress her in the biggest cape or the longest train and she will wear it as if she were born in it. It's exciting and healthy to be around that kind of strength and determination. Superstar may be an overworked term, but not when it applies to Diana Ross.

Then there's **Bette Midler**. Who can safely explain Bette Midler? I can't, so I won't try. She's one hell of a good lady.

Now and then a girl who is just starting out in the business knocks on my door and what a pleasure it is to be in on the beginning of a new career. That's what happened when I was asked to design some special appearance clothes for **Cheryl Ladd** of "Charlie's Angels."

Cheryl is an incredible package of all things that are good! I knew she was a beautiful, natural blonde with a great body, but I had no idea she could sing and dance as well as act. It seems to me there can only be success in Cheryl's future.

My first film experience was with **Debbie Reynolds** in a movie entitled "Divorce, American Style." Debbie was to play the average mother of two, quite a departure for a girl who was always cast as the beautifully gowned ingenue at MGM.

For me, having to design everyday clothes for my first film assignment was more than disappointing, but just getting the job was a thrill. Neither Debbie nor I were terribly excited about the visuals of it all, but we buckled down and proceeded to transform her into the basic lady next door.

Today, I design glamourous gowns and costumes for Debbie's

Diahann Carroll

television and Las Vegas appearances. She is a brilliant impressionist and creating outfits for her Dolly Parton or Charo impressions, among many others, is lots of fun and a far cry from those initial drab beginnings we shared.

Exquisite beauty mixed with talent is a surefire combination, and one of the most beautiful and gifted performers I know is my good friend, **Diahann Carroll**.

Diahann's beauty never gets in her way. She is one of the most down-to-earth, hard-working women I know.

To perform so superbly, to be able to look so incredible and to wear clothes as if she were a professional model, she's got to be in cahoots with the devil. She just keeps getting better, and I never tire of watching her.

Many times, in acts like Mitzi Gaynor's or Juliet Prowse's, performers will change costumes several times during the evening. There are others who prefer to wear the same outfit throughout an entire show. **Chita Rivera**, the dynamic Broadway singer-dancer, came to me a few years ago and requested that I design something she could wear for the whole show without having to leave the stage to change. I finally decided on a simple, halter-neck, jersey jumpsuit with two different jackets, which could be changed right on stage. It turned out to be the perfect solution, and with someone as exciting and talented as Chita, that was all that was needed.

You can learn a great deal from performers if you are secure enough to realize that they, too, have opinions and that you're working together as a team. One lesson I learned very early in my career was that many performers know instinctively what is right for them and what will work best.

A possessor of the true glamour that stars are made of is **Alexis Smith**, who has successfully made the transition from the glamourous days of Hollywood to the Broadway of today. Alexis can mesmerize an audience just by walking onto a stage.

The effervescent **Mary Costa** is a perfect example that opera singers can be slim and beautiful. Always ready for a good laugh and full of exuberance, Mary radiates a quality not usually expected from a peaches-and-cream Southern beauty. She is probably the most glamourous Merry Widow to ever waltz across a stage.

My first meeting with **Barbra Streisand** occurred in 1963, when she was guesting on Judy Garland's weekly television show. At the

Chita Rivera.

Harry Langdon Photography

A design for Chita Rivera.

Mary Costa.

Photo by Stewart Tilger

Alexis Smith.

time, I was working as the assistant designer on the show, which meant having to do anything the designer didn't particularly want to be bothered with.

Barbra was just beginning her incredible career, and at that time she was still considered a curiosity by most people. After that week I could have warned legions of directors, writers and lighting men about her basic lack of trust and her fanatical quest for absolute perfection.

I can still recall that off-white midi-blouse and skirt that Barbra was wearing. To go with them were beautiful, handmade, pure white silk, Italian pumps, which she had personally brought in. My job was to see to it that the shoes were dyed to match the off-white color of her dress. Not trusting anyone else to do this chore, I decided to do it myself. I went to Barbra's dressing room to pick up the shoes, but she was not about to let her prized possession out of her sight. She trotted alongside me all the way down to the CBS wardrobe department, where she advised me on how to mix the exact shade of off-white dye. As I was about to apply the mixture, she grabbed the applicator and dyed her own pumps as I stood by and watched. It was an incident that turned out to be a rather prophetic clue to the nature of the lady.

Seeing those two women, Judy, at the end of her career, and Barbra, just starting out, performing so brilliantly together was a once-in-a-lifetime experience and for me a memory worth saving.

Today Barbra is a true movie star and an exceptional actress, always concerned about the way she looks on camera and completely

Barbra Streisand.

Barbra in a costume from Funny Lady.

aware of the film medium. She has great style and a fine sense of color. She has experimented for a long time, knows what looks good on her and she is usually right. When we were filming *Funny Lady* almost twelve years later, Barbra spent hours in the make-up chair, mixing and matching the exact shades to go with each costume change. Every piece of Art Deco jewelry from her own extensive collection was personally chosen by her to complement each one of the costumes.

She is a perfectionist, and because of it she is sometimes difficult to work with. Yet one cannot but respect her ability and talent. To work with her is always a challenge. A unique personality, Barbra was original when she started and still is!

Every client who comes into my studio has completely different requirements, but I would wager that nobody could ever successfully wear **Carol Channing**'s clothes but Carol.

Carol, like a wonderful, bigger-than-life-size doll, is a tall woman with huge saucer eyes, a large, friendly mouth and the biggest head of blonde hair in the history of hair. Her costumes have to be designed in scale to match her features. Collars must be high, hats the size of turkey platters and buttons never smaller than silver dollars. She hates prints because she maintains that her face is busy enough, but big polka dots and wide stripes are acceptable. Like the characters in the funny papers, Carol wears only pure colors.

In the Broadway show, *Lorelei*, she wore a 1920's wedding gown with thousands of pearl buttons and a matching hat that required two small men just to carry it. Carol walked onto the stage as if she were wearing a simple little tea dress.

Here is a lady who knows what works for her, and it's a pleasure to help her achieve it.

(Left) Carol Channing. (Above) Carol in her button wedding gown.

Photo by Seawell

Photo courtesy of CBS

Barbara Eden and Hans Conreid in a scene from Kismet.

The first time **Barbara Eden** and I worked together was on the television version of the Broadway musical, *Kismet*. Barbara was to play the wildly seductive Lalume, a true vamp. Because of her image as the wholesome, all-American type, I was convinced that she had been hopelessly miscast. Much to my delight, she slinked around in her sexy, Arabian finery fooling us all. Today, Barbara plays all types of roles, but it was fun being in on her first seductress.

It never fails to be a challenge to work with clients who have not as yet established a look for themselves. Either they are very versatile and don't really have a specific look, or they are young and fresh and have not yet decided in what direction their work will take them. This is what happened in 1977 when I was commissioned to design a television wardrobe with a brand-new look for **Marie Osmond**.

Marie was about to turn 18 and everyone concerned felt that she needed a new image. She had started on the series when she was only 14 and had gone through a growing up period, during which she changed from a round little girl into a beautiful, young woman with a lovely figure.

As a role model for the Mormon Church, her family worried that I might turn their little darling into a Hollywood vixen, which was certainly not my intention. Marie had charm and a personality all her own, and it made no sense to try and transform her into a Cher or a Raquel Welch. We had great fun developing a look that was young, sometimes a little crazy, often very pretty and romantic, but, hopefully, always interesting.

At the beginning I designed an outfit with a loose blouson top over straight-legged pants tucked into boots, which resulted in a great deal of high-level discussion about the tightness of Marie's pants. Since Marie has long, well-shaped legs, I naturally preferred having them fit rather snugly. Mother, brothers and any visiting church members who happened to be around were expressing their opinions about the fit of Marie's pants. Marie and I liked them snug, so they more or less agreed, but with a lot of rumbling going on for the rest of the week. The following week I designed a similar outfit and to avoid any more hubbub, we fitted the pants more loosly. On the day of the taping performance, Marie was on stage singing and dancing with Donny when one of her brothers came up to me quite upset that Marie's pants weren't as sharp looking as they had been the previous week. The following week the looser pants were returned to be taken in, and, from then on, till the end of the season, I followed my own judgment on what a hip, young, religious girl singer should wear on television.

Every once in a while someone will come and say to me "Change Me; I want to look different." As a rule, I won't do it. I'm not a makeover artist, and I dislike making someone look like something they are not. If a performer's surface embellishments don't jibe with their inner self, chances are their performances won't either. This goes strictly for personality performers. Actors playing a role should be able to turn themselves, with the help of the proper clothes and make-up, into almost anything. I am happier when performers have an idea about what they want and I'm able to help them turn that idea into a reality. By the time they come to me, most women have a very distinct look and

Marie

Marie Osmond.

personality, and it's my job to improve and enhance what has already been established.

Many people are convinced that I was totally responsible for **Cher**'s television success during the early seventies. This is nonsense. If a performer doesn't have talent to begin with, all the packaging in the world isn't going to help. Cher had a strong look and personality long before we met. As a young girl in the mid-sixties, she was the first personality in the public eye that I know of who wore hip-hugging bell-bottoms, tight T-shirts and long, straight hair, a look that was to become a national uniform for young girls for more than a decade. She was truly a trend setter all on her own.

When Cher came to see me she knew she was ready for a new look. While she wasn't exactly sure what that look should be, she knew it had to be more adult and glamourous. And just as I have helped her achieve that look, Cher helped me in gaining recognition for my work.

I recall our first meeting in 1967. She and Sonny were guesting on the then new Carol Burnett show. In those days, in addition to the regular guests, a youth-oriented rock act was always booked to insure capturing the teenage audience. Sonny and Cher did their number and participated in a *Show Boat* finale. While designing Cher's costume for the finale, I was worried about how this huge, gawky girl would look dressed in ruffles next to Nanette Fabray and Carol Burnett. Well, this huge, gawky girl turned out to be a tiny size six, who looked absolutely charming in her ruffles and twin ponytails. Having always seen her leaning on Sonny's shoulder, I automatically assumed her to be almost six feet tall, not realizing that standing next to Sonny made her appear very tall.

During our work on that show, she admired a beaded gown I had designed. I promised that someday I would design a glamourous beaded gown for her. Well, that day came, and I have since designed more elaborately beaded gowns for Cher than for any woman in the business.

With that incomparable natural ease, and her exquisite face and body, Cher can wear the most exotic and extreme creations without feeling or looking out of place. While her body is long and lean, she has all the required feminine curves that make her so ideal for wearing clothes well. Her head is a perfect oval that sits beautifully on a long, graceful neck. Her features are less than perfect, but for me they combine to make her one of the true beauties of our time. Cher is a master in the art of make-up, and her face is the perfect canvas on which to ply her art. There hasn't been a woman in the limelight since Garbo or Dietrich who could pull off such outrageous visual fantasies while maintaining her individual beauty.

We've had a terrific working relationship and together we've been through a lot, including marriages, shows, divorces, more shows, pregnancy, whatever. Yet Cher remains a straightforward and, on the surface, an uncomplicated girl with a taste for beautiful things, good times, honesty and Dr. Pepper.

Most of the ladies I work with are blessed with great bodies, which often require revealing or, I should say, wild sexy costumes in their line of business. I love the challenge of coming up with new ways to reveal a beautiful body. I believe it was **Tina Turner** who developed the wild "snaky" rag look, and we've had a marvelous time coming up with as many variations of that theme as possible.

Tina is a lady who is harder on her clothes than anyone I know. Her costumes must wear like iron. When performing, she is a wild human dynamo, but in private life she prefers beautifully tailored pants

Photo courtesy of CBS

(Above) Cher in the sixties. (Left) Sonny and Cher guesting on "The Carol Burnett Show" in 1967.

Introducing the Ladies   177

and soft silk shirts with a manner to match. To know the on and off stage Tina is like knowing two completely different people.

Raquel Welch, who possesses one of the most memorable figures of our time, depends on her clothes to help reflect an image of excitement and sensuality. Her body is part of her personality and dressing properly is tremendously important.

Raquel has incredible caramel-colored skin and when dressed in golds and bronzes the total effect is sensational. Her face reflects a catlike beauty, which gives her that predatory sex appeal we're all so familiar with. She is blessed with all the right ingredients, but enhancing them is purely premeditated, down to the last detail. Nobody becomes a major sex symbol by just being there. This lady knows how she wants to look, and she does it successfully.

Ann-Margret is another performer who knows exactly what she wants. Her successful and versatile career has come a long way from her beginnings as a teenage sex symbol. Each year she is on the road with her nightclub act, which is in reality a mini-Broadway show. In films she has succeeded as a dramatic actress, comedienne and musical comedy performer, but most of all she is an appreciative, considerate person and extremely well-liked by the people in the profession.

I recall Ann-Margret years ago with her huge mane of red hair (then her trademark), those spangled micro-minis, boogalooing her little heart out as if the sixties would never end. Today, her hair shorter and wearing easy, graceful clothes, she projects a subtle sex appeal.

I don't know what her next project will be, but I'm sure it will be both different and exciting as she continues to grow as a performer.

Several years ago, on an Andy Griffith television special, I had twelve dancing chorus girls to costume. I was going over the list of girls who were to comprise the ensemble, when the name of a young lady stood out as unusual in a group of Debbies, Susies and Patties. The young lady in question was **Goldie Hawn**.

When that show was taped and the twelve dancers were on stage with Andy, all you really noticed were Andy and Goldie. She had these big, pin-wheel eyes and this crazy smile, and she was out there having such a terrific time that you couldn't help but notice her. Boy, was she noticed! That was her first and last chorus job. It was the mid-sixties and a perfect time for Goldie to be discovered. She was a sort of psychedelic, off-center Twiggy, with a giggle that could start dogs barking.

Today when I design for Goldie, I realize how she has grown and changed. She has become more serious, a wonderful mother and developed into a fine actress. But the one thing that never changes, thankfully, is that gentle wackiness.

(Above) Design for Raquel Welch. (Opposite) Raquel: finished product!

Cheryl Ladd.

Cher
Carter Inaugural Ball
1977

Bob Mackie

Cher

Bob Mackie

Designs for Cher.
(Opposite) Cher.

Bob Mackie

(Opposite) Ann-Margret.

Tina Turner.

Harry Langdon Photography

Diana
Ross

Bob Mackie

Diana

Bob Mackie

(Opposite) Toni Tennille. (Above and right) Designs for Diana Ross. (Overleaf) Diana Ross.

Skrebneski

Harry Langdon Photography

(Above) Leslie Uggams.
(Right) Mitzi Gaynor.

Photo courtesy of Raymax Productions

(Above) Debbie Reynolds.
(Left) Diahann Carroll.

Harry Langdon Photography

Bette Midler.

Harry Langdon Photography

Goldie Hawn and John Ritter having a good time on her special.

A truly satisfying part of my job is watching what happens to some performers between the time they first come to me and later on in their careers. When I met **Eydie Gorme**, she was fighting a constant battle with the scale and I had to design all sorts of clothes that would flatter her slightly fuller figure. I knew that beneath it all there lurked a small body trying to get out. This past year Eydie has worked very hard watching her calories and, presto! A new woman has emerged, one with a sleek figure. What fun it is planning her stage wardrobe now that we can try things that were never possible before.

Eydie has an opening-night tradition. Her husband, Steve Lawrence, never sees any of her new gowns until she walks out on stage. It's her way of surprising him, and she gets great pleasure out of making him proud of the way she looks.

In working with all the top comediennes, I quickly learned two important lessons: funny clothes do not necessarily make for a good comedy act, and comedy can be so fragile that certain clothes can overwhelm wonderfully funny material.

Harry Langdon Photography

(Above) A design for Eydie Gorme. (Left) Eydie and her husband, Steve Lawrence.

The late **Totie Fields**, whose comedy was never timid, used to wear bright, flamboyant costumes on stage, which never seemed to dim her talent. Aside from being one of the most courageous and terrific human beings I've ever known, Totie was a consummate performer, who took great pride in her appearance. At the beginning she was cute and chubby (polite for fat) and loved stage clothes that were wonderfully big and flashy in a rather humorous way. Yet everyone knew Totie didn't need flamboyant costumes to be funny. Totie was a dynamic lady who came on like a gang buster.

When we first met, I was more than a little overwhelmed; in fact, I felt she was a little too strong for me to deal with. Once she was quite audibly unhappy about some detail on a gown, and I felt she was wrong. I answered her just as loudly and watched this tiny dynamo completely wilt before my very eyes. From that time on, I never felt intimidated by Totie; in fact, she will always remain a very special lady in my life.

(Above) A design for Totie Fields.
(Right) Totie.

Photo by Gene Howard, Studio Five Inc.

Photo courtesy of CBS

Designing for a group usually means creating one design that will look good on everyone. Not so with the **Pointer Sisters**.

These exquisite, tall, black women have three very distinct personalities and looks. They prefer to look like individuals and designing for them is like working with three different stars. The girls are known for their clothes as well as their music, so for me it's a great opportunity to come up with the most bizarre and entertaining gowns possible. They have an innate style that enables them to wear the most wonderful clothes, no matter how wild.

It's always a thrill when ladies will travel half way across the world to have me design for them. Recently, **Sylvie Vartan**, the famous French singer-dancer, asked me to create costumes to enhance her exotic blonde beauty. Imagine the thrill of arriving in Paris to find posters of Sylvie wearing my designs plastered all over town.

(Above) The Pointer Sisters.

Harry Langdon Photography

(Above) Pia Zadora.
(Opposite) Sylvie Vartan.

Pia Zadora, a five-foot bundle of energy, is another new and exciting client of mine. Pia has been in show business a good many years for one so young. Having started as a child on the Broadway stage, she has accumulated a fund of experience, which makes for a polished performer. In spite of her diminutive size, she has a wildly sexy body for which it is a pleasure to design.

On the opposite end of the height scale is the statuesque six-foot blonde beauty, **Susan Anton**, who sings as beautifully as she looks. Susan, you may remember, is the Muriel Cigar Girl, who sends men's hearts aflutter. A body that long calls for the most dramatic designs and, of course, I don't mind that at all.

Some years ago, a strangely charming little girl with the face of a Victorian angel and a "Pretty Girl" body came into my life. Dressed in a Joan Crawford suit, platform wedgies and a head full of Betty Grable curls, she arrived carrying a straw bag containing scuffed tap shoes and a fluffy little dog named Rocco. **Bernadette Peters**, who had just arrived from New York, fresh from the off-Broadway production of *Dames At Sea*, completely captivated me with her crackly child's voice and absolutely straightforward, honest enthusiasm. Today, after much experience and great acclaim, she's still the hard-working, charming, little girl I first met years ago.

Bernadette has always had that quality of being from another time and place, with a face and body that can evoke the twenties, thirties or forties. But for me she is at her best portraying a beauty from the turn of the century, and I dream of some day designing a show starring Bernadette as "The Gibson Girl."

One of our all-American beauties is the former Miss America, sportscaster **Phyllis George**, who is just now beginning to expose her performing talents, along with her contest-winning figure. She is a triple-threat girl in the world of show business, and I am looking forward to packaging her, one of our great natural resources.

Actually the first girl I designed for in my career and in hers was singer **Vikki Carr**. We both attended Rosemead High School in California, and I created designs for her when she was fifteen and I was sixteen. We were both very active in high school theatrics and today love to reminisce about the good old days at RHS. Vikki has remained a good friend and certainly a most loyal client.

Watching **Leslie Uggams** on television's "Name That Tune" show when I was thirteen years old and she was even younger, I certainly never in my wildest dreams imagined that I would one day create

Photo by Michael Childers

Harry Langdon Photography

Vikki Carr.

Harry Langdon Photography

Phyllis George.

Harry Langdon Photography

Photo by Francesco Scavullo

(Above and right) Bernadette Peters.
(Opposite) Susan Anton.

Jaye P. Morgan

glamourous creations for that skinny, smart, little kid.

Today she sings as beautifully as ever, but also has proven herself to be a brilliant actress. If one looks past today's glamour, there's still the same winning smile and sparkling eyes of that skinny, little kid I saw on that TV show so many years ago.

One singer who's never a problem to design for is **Abbe Lane**. While she is performing, the temperature rises as she sizzles her way through a repertoire of exciting numbers. Because of her copper hair and year-round tan, I love to dress her in copper, coral, brown or white, all hues that emphasize her unique coloring. Besides being a wonderful performer, Abbe is always a most considerate and appreciative woman.

The unpredictable **Jaye P. Morgan** is hardly your run-of-the-mill singer. Since she never stands still for one second, her gowns must move and expose plenty of leg. As far as color goes, we've never gotten past white, red or orange; these always seem to do the trick. She will spend countless hours in the fitting room, posing and practicing with a gown to see what different looks she can achieve with a single design. For, once again, the dresses must work their way through a solid hour of various songs and moods.

Toni Tennille is a sexy, chic and glamourous woman. This wasn't always apparent, and so I was delighted when we decided to work together to give Toni a sophisticated look to match her new music.

When Toni and the Captain did their TV special, "The Captain and Tennille Songbook, they were looking for a different approach. Happily, reviewers reported that she had acquired not only a new visual image, but also a more discriminating audience.

Toni is a positive lady. She's also one of the most organized, cooperative and disciplined performers I've ever known.

As you have probably guessed, designing for singing stars can be the hardest task of all. They may stand in one dress for an hour, singing an assortment of songs that convey a variety of moods and emotions. Their gowns must enhance rather than overpower their performance. The gown's color is important as it must be flattering and able to look well under many different colored lights and effects. While white or a light color is always the most successful, there are times, especially if the performer is blonde or particularly dynamic, when black looks marvelous. The lighting man, of course, hates black, since any color he casts on it always remains black. Each season I work hard to try and come up with new variations on gowns for stand-up singers.

(Opposite) Abbe Lane.

Photo by Francesco Scavullo

Each year has brought new challenges and new performers into my life. But throughout most of my career there has always been one constant: **Carol Burnett**.

I worked with Carol on her weekly comedy-variety show for eleven years and can't think of anyone I would rather have spent the time with. She is a very special woman. She has helped me grow, and I have been fortunate enough to be around watching her as she has developed into the performer she is today. We now know each other so well that we can almost read each others' minds. This, of course, leads to a good working relationship.

When I was first hired to do Carol's show, I had always been a fan, but we had never met. At our first meeting, at which I was somewhat nervous, to say the least, I showed her some sketches. I arrived at her house with about twenty drawings I felt she would look good in. She greeted me at the door with the same warmth and down-to-earth charm that America's television audiences love. After we both nervously went through the sketches, she exclaimed that she loved them all,

Stella Toddler

Eunice

Mrs. Wiggins

winked and asked me if I had ever thought in terms of an older woman! From that point on I knew I loved her.

What I think I remember most about our work together over the years are all the classic characters that Carol created. We would share ideas each week in order to come up with the best possible look for each of her 'ladies.' I particularly remember the development of the vague secretary, Mrs. Wiggins. The script called for Mrs. Wiggins to be a small, elderly lady with a gray bun and glasses. I was bored with the idea of another little, old lady character, so I suggested to Carol that we make her just the opposite of what the name implied. She became the useless girl one finds in every large office, whose sole purpose in life is to dress as sexy as possible and be in the elevator at the stroke of 5:00 P.M. From those ideas came the awful blonde hair, the sleazy print blouse and the very tight black skirt. I designed the costume, Carol designed the wiggle, and Mrs. Wiggins was created.

Carol always put a lot of thought into her characterizations, but none of them were created with the idea of becoming regular members of her repertoire. If they were funny and got the proper reception, they were invited back, but when they ceased to be funny the invitation was withdrawn. I never knew if a costume I was designing would be on one show only or if it would keep reappearing week after week. That's what happened when Eunice was created. She was written as a Tennessee Wiliams-type lady. To me she was Blanche DuBois with a little Minnie Pearl thrown in. I found a 1930's print chiffon dress in a thrift shop, shortened the skirt, redraped the bodice, added a pair of hideous white sandals, and with the perfect hairdo, Eunice was born! Carol and the audience fell in love with poor old Eunice and kept inviting her back. The only problem was the fragile dress began falling apart. We tried to duplicate it, but Carol felt a certain loyalty to the old original, so we just kept patching it.

In eleven years the amount of comedy that Carol has performed boggles the mind. She can play the most subtle humor or pull out all the stops. She is an incredible comic and an amazing lady. In fact, during the first year of her show she amazed me with a first in my career. About halfway through the season, I began to notice that she was putting on a little weight. I casually mentioned it to her one day, and she gave me some lame excuse about an occasional beer before bedtime to help her sleep. Now really! A few weeks later she was doing a Southern belle number in which she was to drop her hoop skirt to reveal her pantal-lettes. The skirt dropped and I gasped. The tight bodice had squeezed her tummy out into rather questionable proportions. I headed to the technical booth to talk to our producer, Joe Hamilton, who I was sure would have the answer since he's also Carol's husband. Joe just laughed. My suspicions were confirmed. Carol was indeed pregnant with their third child. They wanted to keep it a secret so that the audience wouldn't worry about her condition as she was going through her weekly slapstick routines. I explained that they could keep their secret a lot longer if they would let the costume designer in on it! So yours truly had his first experience concealing a pregnancy. I did it twice during the Carol Burnett show for Vicki Lawrence and a few years ago costumed Cher for almost five months while she performed and awaited the arrival of her second child. I am now proud to say that I've become an expert at spotting early pregnancies. They can't fool me anymore.

Carol's show is now over, and while I'll miss the weekly routine, I know we will continue to work on projects together. I am happy to see Carol moving forward into new directions and making full use of her unlimited talents.

Well, here we are on page 207. I've had a terrific time letting you in on some of my ideas and trade secrets. I know that you can make them work for you. Now get your new, glamourous self together and go out and conquer your world!